The Truth Behind My Trident

Overcoming Life and Business Obstacles
the Navy SEAL Way

Phillip W. Koontz

With Beth Tancredi

CONTENTS

DEDICATION

To my amazing friends and family who have unconditionally loved and supported me throughout my life's successes and hardships. Words cannot express how grateful I am.

DISCLAIMER

The perspective and opinions expressed in this book do not reflect those of the entire Naval Special Warfare community. My personal involvement and views are unique to my service in the Navy and are not a direct reflection of every SEAL's experience.

PREFACE

I calculated out that the actual amount of operational time we spend performing our jobs (on a mission, for example) is around 2.7% of our entire two-year training cycles. Not including sleep and time off on weekends, we spend roughly 97.3% of our waking hours training and preparing for war.

And Hollywood highlights our missions which, again, comprise only a small amount of our time.

Why am I bringing this up?

Because the other 97.3% of the time looks much different than the missions portrayed in the movie theaters.

That is one of the purposes of this book... to simply attempt to pull back the curtain and show what a day in the life of a SEAL looks like.

The Go Bag

Whether you've decided to read my book because you've seen me at one of my speaking engagements or you picked it up because you have an interest in books about the military, it is important to me that you walk away from this with more than just a story about the life of a Navy SEAL.

If that's all you get out of my story, then I haven't done my job.

My goal here is to make sure that you are equipped for properly navigating your way through your everyday life or mission – in a nutshell, to help you accomplish your goals – using my military experience as a metaphor.

Trackin' thus far?

See, when I was overseas, we all had our own "Go" Bags. These bags held both our defensive and offensive gear that we needed to successfully accomplish our missions.

Go Bags, however, should not be limited to those in the military. Everyone should have one – whether it's physical, spiritual or emotional – that is filled with the tools for your own personal success.

Consider the items in my Go Bag:

- **Kevlar helmet**: What do you have in your Go Bag that will help protect your mind from negativity or self-defeating thoughts?

- **Body armor**: What do you have in your Go Bag that will help protect your heart and vital organs - the essence of who you are? What components have you set in place to protect the essence of who you are against the onslaught of cultural norms of busyness, hyper-productivity, results over relationships, "microwave culture" (I want it now), a "feel-good" culture, materialism = keeping up with the Joneses, etc.?

- **H-Gear**: My body armor fits inside my H-gear, but H-gear also has pockets for radios, magazines, grenades, medical supplies, etc. What are you equipping yourself with that will not only protect your vital organs (like the body armor), but also help you offensively fight back? This could be your faith, church, friends, hobbies, family, etc.

- **Boots**: What do you have in your Go Bag that will help you persevere – taking one step at a time?

- **My uniform**: My uniform is my second skin. Are you comfortable in your own skin? Do you really know who you are? Is your identity intact and solid? If not, you will waffle insecurely and drift to whichever way your peers or the culture is currently influencing you.

- **Helo (helicopter) Lanyard**: A helo lanyard is a one-inch piece of nylon fabric with a bungee cord inside. One end attaches to the operator's rigger belt and the other end attaches to the D-ring on the floor of the helicopter. This simple piece of gear prevents the person from falling out of the helicopter. What in your Go Bag has you securely fastened in order to provide the grounding you need when the storms of life come? What will anchor you during the turbulent storms of life?

- **Ammunition**: What in your Go Bag do you have to incapacitate the enemies around you? As Navy SEALs, we put certain rounds in our weapons in order to accomplish the mission or task in front of us. What ammunition do you use and is it effective against the enemies of fear, shame, gossip, rumors, slander, pride, lust, greed, etc.?

As you read through my story, don't just think of what I have done to persevere in my life and career. Think about how you can do the same with the right tools.

CHAPTER 1

A Warrior in the Making

Embrace the warrior within you. Don't hide it or deny it, but instead, give it an outlet.

I love weapons.

That shouldn't be a surprise to you coming from a former Navy SEAL or frogman.

Ever since I can remember, I would spend hours in my father's workshop fashioning weapons of all sorts.

Homemade knives. Bows and arrows made of branches. Throwing stars, nunchucks, swords, slingshots. You name it.

Now, before you start worrying about the mental stability of the guy writing this book, I will tell you (*and moms of sons can easily attest*) that this is completely normal for young boys. I believe God made all boys with built-in sound effects (which totally makes playing better and more realistic) and the innate sense to battle.

Just about *any* household item or gift from mother nature can – and will – be turned into a weapon by a boy if given the opportunity.

Give them that opportunity. It doesn't mean they are violent or will grow up and do awful things, it simply means they are being boys.

As a boy, when my arsenal was complete, I would suit up and parade around the neighborhood defending it from the "bad guys." Only, the bad guys I was beating up were trees and bushes.

I remember building forts in the woods about a mile away from my house and sneaking around my neighborhood with mud on my face while I hunted and trapped birds, raccoons and squirrels.

That was my kind of adventure.

I swear I was also the only kid in elementary school who wore camouflaged clothes to school ... All. The. Time.

So much so, that my peers would make fun of me by calling me "G.I. Joe."

Did they think that offended me? Pssh!

Hell, no! It made me smile inside.

So, I guess you could say I have had a warrior brewing inside me since I was young. *Those of you reading this book who can resonate with this... embrace the warrior within you. Don't hide it or deny it, but instead give it an outlet.*

Well, not much has changed.

I still love weapons – but they are big boy toys now. Real knives, guns, grenades, flash bangs, LAW rockets, Carl

Gustavs, AT-4s, .50 Cals, automatic grenade launches, claymore mines, limpet mines, C-4 explosives, chainsaws, machine guns ... you name it.

And this time, the "bad guys" actually fight back.

Around the age of 12, I needed a channel for my pent-up energy. Oddly enough, I found that outlet in competitive swimming.

My 12-year old feet scratched against the grainy block as I shifted my weight back and forth. I took a deep breath of the chlorine-filled air and then got into position, bent over and readied for the start. My heart beat in what felt like hurried, loud explosions and my breath echoed in my head as I waited for the buzzer to signal the start.

"This race is mine," I thought as the starting buzzer sounded.

Competitive swimming taught me discipline. It taught me that determination, perseverance, and hard work pay off.

I confess, sometimes I took that perseverance thing too far. My desire to push myself beyond my capabilities was so intense that it wasn't unusual for me to throw up in my mouth in the middle of a lap – and hold it in until I reached the gutter at the end of the lane. My modus operandi was the "spit and flip" at the end of the lane just to keep going during the race. My "record," for lack of a better word, was throwing up four times in a single practice.

Practice. Not even a race.

Looking back on it, I guess that should have been the indicator that I was approaching hardcore challenges much different than most.

My passion for swimming brought me to the University of Toledo, where I was awarded a scholarship and swam Division I for the Rockets. My swimming career at Toledo scored many awards for myself and the team.

During that time, I placed in the 100- and 200-meter backstroke and 200-meter freestyle in the MidAmerican Conferences. Both years, in fact, our team placed second in those conferences.

Competitive swimming taught me to graciously welcome victory and to humbly accept defeat. But most importantly, it was an introduction to a brotherhood of sorts.

My initiation into the brotherhood was hardly pleasant. And I knew that being accepted into it might require me to put aside some pride and do some rather – ahem - unpleasant things.

"You want me to swallow WHAT?" I asked my team captain as he held up a clear plastic baggie with goldfish swimming around inside.

Just like that, I felt it welling up inside me. I'm not sure if it was liquid courage, my own machismo or a combination of both, but I rose (no, I jumped) to the occasion.

"Hell yeah! I'll take two!" I proudly said, and promptly threw two live fish in my mouth, chewed them up and swallowed them. (And by the way, I did it faster than anyone. Yeah, I'm a little competitive.)

My band of brothers hooted and hollered at my accomplishment and picked me up for my first collegiate keg stand to wash the taste of goldfish out of my mouth.

That may have been my first initiation into a brotherhood. Little did I know then, it wasn't going to be my last.

And with every race and every phase of my life, I'd push my body harder and harder to best my competitors and myself. My soul was in the water and my body was merely the vehicle I used to express my passion for it.

I had no idea that I was a SEAL in the making.

In my second year at the University of Toledo, the rumor mill began to churn with whispers that the school was doing away with their men's swimming program.

It was time to rethink. Time to recalculate my course.

At this point, I had to face two realities:

1- Let's face it, Michael Phelps, I wasn't. Neither physically nor genetically. I was never going to make a living as a competitive swimmer, and

2- My girlfriend was living in Cincinnati.

So, I hung up my suit, packed my bags and headed down to Oxford, Ohio to start my new life at Miami University. It was time to focus on my future.

By 2001, I married my first wife, Erin, and picked up some shifts at the Olive Garden as a server to make ends meet.

Like most college students, I wasn't quite sure what I wanted to do when I grew up, but as a people-person with a personality for sales, a marketing degree made the most sense to me.

In 2002, I received my Bachelor's Degree in marketing, walked off that stage and practically climbed right on board the plane to Connecticut, to a company called News Marketing America in Wilton, Connecticut.

I was thrilled to take on the world!

Erin and I rented a home that was just shy of being the white picket fenced house that you tend to picture when you think of small-town America. Everything about it was ideal, perfect New England.

But all was not perfect.

Little did I realize the corporate world was **mind numbing**.

Day after day, I sat in my cubicle making phone calls to clients and sending emails in an effort to drum up business for the in-store printed coupon promotional media. You know it's bad when your favorite part of the day is lunch. During lunch, I'd sit at my computer, put my headphones on and lose myself in my music.

I may not have been built for a career in competitive swimming, but I also wasn't built for this. I was built for more than the hum-drum day-to-day with characters whose spirits were equally squelched by aisles of cubes as far as the eye could see.

It was pathetic. And I knew I was going nowhere fast. I was too impatient to climb the corporate ladder to the position I was promised would be mine in roughly four years.

I can't tell you how many times I was struck by that reality – and the reality that if I didn't make a move soon, I would be in my mid-40s staring in the face of my midlife crisis before I knew it.

I needed something new. Different. Inspired. Intense.

I first considered joining the police force in Westport, Connecticut. I started the interview process and made it all the way down to the final two candidates, but my response to a single question brought my candidacy to a screeching halt.

"What will you do if you don't get the position with us?" I was asked.

"I'll join the military. Special forces." I responded.

Maybe that wasn't the reason I was turned down for the job. But no matter. It was divine intervention.

Now, at this time, my wife was growing uncomfortable with the thought of being married to someone exploring such dangerous careers. And despite much counseling, we never mastered the art of conflict resolution.

So, at 22-years-old, I found myself reading a "Dear John" letter from my wife, saying she had moved back to Cincinnati (our home town) to live with her parents. I was stunned, scared and lost all at the same time. At least she left me the dog.

Per Ohio law, you cannot file for divorce until you have lived in the state for six months. And no sooner had six months passed, then I was served with my divorce papers.

At that point, I was holed up with some friends in Westport, working as a Shift Supervisor at Starbucks.

Little did I know, I was seven months away from shipping out to boot camp.

The military was calling me. I knew in my heart and soul that the armed forces would scratch that itch – that intensity – that I needed to have a fulfilling life.

I first went to the Army recruiter in 2003, fueled down the narrow hallway of the recruiting office by posters that boasted men in camouflage, wielding weapons. Army boats. Big guns. Men in ghillie suits. I was ready to be that man. I was where I was supposed to be.

But at 22, I was still a bit of a cocky college graduate who had no interest in the two-year requirement to serve in the infantry before I could ever even consider the Army's special forces program.

I left the Army recruiting office and decided to make one last stop across the hall – Navy.

No sooner had I crossed that threshold was I met by Sean, the recruiter, who was nothing less than the epitome of a Navy salesman. During our conversation, Sean hit on every sentiment and buzzword that assured me that this was truly the right fit for me. And as it turns out, Sean was a rock star at his job – he was the number one Naval Special Warfare recruiter on the entire East Coast.

The option to join the Navy was, in my mind, the perfect fit. I loved to swim. I loved the water. I could go immediately into boot camp, followed by A School for my technical training and then immediately into Basic Underwater Demolition SEAL (BUD/S). And let's face it, the $8,000 sign-on bonus simply because I had my college degree didn't hurt.

And just when I thought the stars couldn't align any more than they already had, in walks a man named "Rob" (I won't use his real name to protect his identity). A man with intensity that matched mine, Rob was a triathlete who had competed in several Ironman competitions and had travelled all the way from Florida to Bridgeport, Connecticut to sign up for the SEALs under my rock star recruiter, Sean.

We hit it off immediately. Without even a second thought, Rob suggested that I move down to Florida with his brother and mother to train together for the four months prior to going to boot camp. He needed help with his swimming, and I needed help with running. We developed our own kind of brotherhood, that followed us from that recruiting office, to Florida and then through the same boot camp, BUD/S class, SEAL team, task unit and platoon. That is unheard of and extremely rare.

I shipped out for boot camp in March 2004.

Now, I would be remiss if I didn't mention that prior to heading down to Florida was a time when my faith in God deepened. I visited church regularly as part of my spiritual journey to figure out who I was and what I should be doing.

You may have heard the saying, "If you place your heart in God's hands He will place your heart in the hands of a worthy person." That could not have been truer for me. Because it was at church in 2003 where I met my second wife, Danielle.

She embodied everything I was looking for: spiritual, independent, compassionate, thoughtful, beautiful and tender.

Our courtship was short, sweet and intense, and we married the following July.

CHAPTER 2

Pulling Back the Curtain

It's not how far you can push yourself, but how you respond at your breaking point.

As we have all seen, war and military strategy today is far different than it has been in years past. With today's intelligence, technology and equipment, we're really dealing with something that's "not your father's war."

I have been told that ever since the George W. Bush Administration, Congress has been more aggressively trying to push recruits through Basic Underwater Demolition/ SEAL school (BUD/S) in order to address the unconventional needs of today's military strategy. These forces are the new version of "boots on the ground" who can offer the more effective and increasingly common surgical strikes that lead to victory.

To support these needs, Congress has spent millions of dollars trying to identify the traits of the people who can succeed in these roles given such demands in order to strategically focus their recruiting efforts.

Despite hiring a multitude of researchers and psychologists, these efforts to identify the right people for the right job have largely been unsuccessful. They have, however, identified a couple of traits:

1- The two sports that most SEALs participated in through high school and or college were swimming and wrestling.

2- Many SEALs come from the Midwest.

Being from Cincinnati, Ohio and a competitive swimmer for 12 years, I fell neatly into both categories.

So, what is it about swimmers that puts them among the most apt candidates for special forces? In my opinion, it is because we push ourselves so hard and are accustomed to a grueling swim schedule of two practices a day nearly year-round.

A common question I get asked is whether SEAL training is more demanding mentally or physically. By far it is more mentally demanding. I would say my training process was 80% mental and 20% physical. See, it is only a matter of time until the body breaks from the physical stress and at that point, the instructors want to see if you have what it takes mentally to push through despite your physical brokenness, pain and exhaustion.

Now obviously, it takes more qualities to be a successful SEAL than those identified by researchers. And to be honest, even as someone who personally coaches and trains candidates for BUD/S, it's even hard for me to tell whether someone will make it or not based on physical appearances. It's often an intuitive knowledge that tells me who will be successful.

The History Channel recently released a list of the top characteristics that former SEALs say help determine success on the Teams. Those traits are:

- Competitive
- Confident
- Decisive
- Determined
- Loyal
- Selfless
- Organized
- Detail-oriented

What I can tell you is that we are a breed of our own. We are trained to endure the atrocities of bloodshed and war. We are determined, hard core, persevering, focused and disciplined to the nth degree. We can't and won't ever quit in the face of adversity, moving forward, gaining ground and fighting until our last breath.

In fact, having been immersed in the life as a "Team Guy," we become pretty good at spotting our brothers out and about town.

There's just a certain something – a very subtle demeanor – that screams out to those of us in the know that someone is a silent warrior. It's the way we carry ourselves. Confident, even arrogant, in the eyes of some.

Once we lock eyes, we give a slight nod and grin, and carry on about our business.

What you often don't see, nor could anyone outside of the brotherhood probably ever identify with, is an inner struggle that is locked deep within our hearts.

For me, that inner struggle intensified when I was dealt the news that my bride, Danielle, was diagnosed with stage four breast cancer only six months after we married.

I remember the day Danielle was diagnosed as if it was yesterday. We were sitting in the doctor's office when he delivered the news. The cancer had started in her breast and had metastasized to her sternum and 26 of her lymph nodes from her waist up.

There I was again – terrified, lost, alone and feeling defeated.

Four years later, she tragically lost her battle with the disease.

My faith in God, which had always been something I could rely on, was shaken. I was emotionally hurting, grappling with life and wandering a bit. Lost, I went to visit our command's psychologist to talk through my feelings. We shared a common faith in God and were able to unpack the type of emotions over life and death that are typically only reserved for moments when bullets are whizzing by your head.

His faith and encouragement were exactly what I needed, giving me what I like to refer to as one of my many "Come to Jesus" moments.

"Phillip," the commander said to me, "What do you think is the most common characteristic that I've seen in Team Guys?"

A whirlwind of characteristics went through my mind. Toughness. Pride. Mental fortitude.

But I didn't say any of those. "I don't know, what?" I asked instead.

"Loneliness," he said.

I was dumbfounded.

You may be asking, *"But Phillip, I thought the SEALs were a close-knit brotherhood. How is it possible to be lonely in that environment?"*

Crazy, right? Most SEALs themselves don't even recognize that they are lonely, and if they do, there is a big fear that acknowledging it would give the appearance of being weak. So, they sit in quiet isolation, on their own island, their feelings never to be exposed, discussed or shared.

The only exception I have come across – the only time that any raw feelings start to surface – is when there is a long enough lull in a firefight that the adrenaline starts to subside. In these rare moments, it feels somehow permissible to be vulnerable, and acceptable to allow any thoughts and feelings out of our guarded cages.

I have both seen and experienced this loneliness in the Teams. We're badass tough guys though, so we do a great job of hiding it and use the outward appearance of our brute strength to masque the pain.

Many Team guys I have known – and I include myself in this group to some degree – are avoiding the pain of our pasts and our dysfunctional or traumatic upbringings that helped drive us to the point we're at today.

I would venture to say that many SEALS who go through the program just want to know if they are really men. Many of us have never heard our fathers tells us we're good enough or that we even have what it takes. So, we look to the SEALS training as the ultimate test to prove that we ARE men and that we DO have what it takes.

I have had many conversations with guys who have joined for that very reason. Somehow, they thought, "Surely, if I can make it through this, I am a man."

But, if I'm being honest, we are rarely convinced even then. What it means to be a man resides deep within. Deeper than any accomplishment or achievement. It is found in our faith. It is found in our sacrifice for our loved ones, our dedication to what is right, and our desire to put others first – above our own selfish desires and motives. To be a man is to pursue what is noble, honorable and true no matter what the cost.

On a side note, if you are reading this book and you are contemplating becoming a SEAL, I encourage you to do some deep soul searching to determine what your true motivations are for wanting to sign up for the program. Do you have something to prove to yourself or someone else?

See, there are two types of people in this world: sheep and sheepdogs. Warriors and everyone else. Every true Frogman knows he's a warrior. That mentality simply does not go away no matter how hard we may try to push it aside or how old we get. With each passing year, each passing phase of our lives, it's there. It just manifests itself in a different way year after year.

The fight is still in us. The intense desire to do something that very few can do – to make a difference in this world, to live for something bigger than ourselves and to physically and mentally push beyond our limits – never goes away.

Unfortunately (or in some cases, fortunately), I will wrestle with this inner tug-of-war for the rest of my life.

If you were ever to see me at the gym, you'd see it for sure. I work out at least five days a week to decompress and give "the fight" an outlet. I normally lift weights or do a Crossfit-type strength training for nearly an hour before transitioning into a full hour of cardio. I become so intensely focused that I often don't even notice the grunts, groans and growls that I'm spewing. In a sense, I guess you could say I exercise to exorcize.

I'm sure, by the way, that there is some clinical diagnosis for this. And if you know of one, please let me know!

But ultimately, it is this inner drive that compels us to continue living a purposeful and driven life.

Let me give you a real-life example. Recently, I contacted The History Channel with an idea for a documentary called "From SEALS to Summit" where they follow former SEALS up K2 or Everest. Did I pitch the idea because I wanted to be famous? Because I wanted to be on TV? Of course not!

I pitched my idea to The History Channel because I was looking for another reason to push myself – my body, my mind and my soul – to the limits. I wanted to know that I still have what it takes. I suppose, in essence, it was another test to prove to myself that I could mentally and physically push myself to the extreme.

Now, this idea for the show may be just a whim. It may pass (when I'm 80?). It may not. Until then, I'll be looking for new ways to challenge myself.

So that's part of what the mind and spirit of a SEAL looks like.

To really know a SEAL though, it also helps to know what a day in the life of a Navy SEAL looks like.

I think that people have this picture that Navy SEALs are constantly shooting weapons, blowing things up, diving, jumping out of aircrafts, in the water or hunting terrorists. Yeah, we do all that. But there's so much more downtime, behind-the-scenes work, preparation for our trips and logistics than one would think. To put it simply, it's not nearly as sexy or glamorous as Hollywood has made it out to be.

However, Hollywood has done a very good job of portraying a certain aspect of the SEALs team. While there are many aspects of that view that are true and realistic, they have not done a great job of painting the true, behind-the-scenes picture of what the life entails.

Upon showing up to a Team, you are issued an 8x10 "cage" that becomes our own personal sanctuaries for storing your gear, PMS (Personal Maintenance), preparing for upcoming training blocks, hanging flags and putting up pictures of loved ones – things that turn "cage" more into "home."

To call it home is a euphemism though, because the reality is that these are cold, metallic caves with concrete floors that allow us to escape and have some quiet. Some guys, especially the single guys or the married men who were in the proverbial doghouse and had nowhere else to go, put up hammocks for sleeping.

Most Teams are divided into Task Units and each Task Unit is further broken down into platoons. Even-numbered teams are sent to the East Coast, while odd-numbered teams are sent to the West Coast.

So, when I showed up to Team 10 in Little Creek, Virginia, we had three Task Units (TU1, TU2 and TU3) each with two platoons. Alpha and Bravo Platoon fell under TU1, Charlie and Delta were part of TU2 and Echo and Foxtrot were under TU3. I was placed in TU3 in Foxtrot Platoon.

I have heard, by the way, that each Team has around 120 SEALS. That was roughly the case for Team 10.

Every morning, each platoon would gather in their own platoon "hut" to eat, hang out, gossip or haze the new guys. (I'll talk more about hazing later in this chapter.)

There are two offices in the platoon hut – one for the Platoon Chief, the head enlisted person in charge of the entire platoon of men, and the other is for the Officer in Charge (OIC). Both men share equal responsibility for the men in their platoons. They are the leaders, the counselors, gate keepers, referees and logistical planners (among other things) for the approximately 16 misfits who are under them. There is also usually one "newer" officer assigned to the platoon who is mentored by the OIC. In all, there are about 14 enlisted men that make up each platoon.

Like your "cage," each Platoon Hut can be decorated however the team wants. The only exception is that the Navy SEAL creed is located on the wall of each and every platoon space. This serves as a reminder to each and every one of us why we are there.

Earn Your Trident Every Day

U.S. Navy SEAL Code

Loyalty to Country, Team, and Teammate
Serve with Honor and Integrity, on and off the Battlefield
Ready to lead, ready to follow, never quit
Take responsibility for your actions, and the actions of your Teammates
Excel as Warriors through Discipline and Innovation
Train for war, fight to win, defeat our Nation's Enemies

The ground floor of my team building included a quarterdeck (the entrance), a hanger bay large enough to hold ceremonial events, work on HUMMVs or boats, or for the team to work out. You would also find the rows and rows of our personal cages on the first floor. Our platoon huts were upstairs. With the exception of pictures of fallen brothers, quotes and memories, the walls of the building were plain white.

Regardless of whether you are stationed with the Naval Special Warfare Amphibious Commands on the East Coast in Little Creek, Virginia or on the West Coast in Coronado, California, your nose and lungs are always filled with salty air.

SEAL teams generally operate on two-year cycles. The first six months, you're in school, followed by another six months of pre-deployment work up. The next six months is our deployment, followed by another six months of schooling, rest, relaxation and decompressing from our time down range.

Typically, once you show up or report to your team, you start with several months of schools. Under normal circumstances, you are assigned to a specific school based on the needs of the platoon. Schools included Communications, Sniper, Medic, Combat Medical Emergency and Trauma, Corpsman (18 Delta), JTAC (for guys calling in air support), Dive Supervisor, HRST Master School, Free Fall school, Lead Climber school, SERE, Defensive Driving, Breacher, etc.

The timing of my arrival, however, was anything but typical or normal.

On June 28, 2005, shortly before I showed up, the SEALs had just lost 11 heroes during Operation Red Wing. It was the greatest loss of life to that date in the history of the Teams.

This tragic loss meant that Team 10 needed to fill a number of spaces. Breacher school had many spots to fill, so I volunteered to go. I lucked out because most "new guys" just showing up to a team don't get offered the "sexier" schools.

After attending Lead Breacher School, Advanced Breacher School and a "home explosives" course run by the CIA, I was then qualified to be one of the main Lead Breachers in my platoon.

As Lead Breachers, our job is to get our brothers on target as quickly and efficiently as possible. From lock picking, quickie saws, chainsaws, sledge hammers, hulie tools, shotguns and torches that burn at 10,000 degrees Fahrenheit, slap charges and other explosive charges, we got to play with it all.

The subsequent six months consist of "work-ups" or pre-deployment work that requires us to travel throughout the United States as a task unit to train in different environments and geographic regions so we can be a well-oiled machine no matter where we find ourselves deployed. So, you could find us in Florida during our diving block of training, Arkansas for land warfare, Alaska for cold-weather training, Nevada for high altitude HUMMV training, Kentucky for MOUNT (or urban) training, etc.

Next up is deployment. At this point in our training, each team and task unit are sent to different "theaters" of the world. There are five theaters in all: The West Coast teams go to PACOM (Pacific Theater), CENCOM (Middle East Theater) and SOUTHCOM (Central and South America Theater), while the East Coast Teams go to EUCOM (European Theater), AFRICOM (African Theater) and CENCOM.

Finally, we return home for the last six months for some rest and relaxation, decompression time, leave (or vacation) and more schools.

To be honest, I have seen this rigorous two-year, 540-day cycle tear apart even the most solid families and marriages.

Want to know a scary statistic? The attrition rate of BUD/S is nearly the same as the divorce rate in the Teams. A whopping 80-90%!

And that failure doesn't discriminate. The stress that this training imposes simply doesn't care who you are, where you come from, or how well you'll deal with it.

Most guys enter with the rank of E-3 or E-4, but this is largely dependent on whether they have a college degree or prior service in the Navy. My understanding, by the way, is that close to 50% of enlisted SEALs have a Bachelor's degree at the very least.

The younger guys – generally ages 19-24 – are often cocky and full of themselves. Bulletproof.

And as I'm sure you probably already guessed, a majority of Team Guys have Type A personalities – hard-chargers who have a difficult time "turning it off." While SEAL Teams thrive with these personality types on board, it made it difficult for people like me – who are not Type A – to fit in or relate at times.

You see, the SEAL teams tend to operate on a wolf pack mentality. It's this very powerful mentality that drives us to succeed, excel and accomplish things that no man could possibly dream of.

But that wolf pack mentality translates into something that is, unfortunately, very much like a high school locker room in which the "good ol' boys' club" strongly prevails.

There is a fine line between being a part of the brotherhood in which you act and sound like one another and simply having one another's back in war (i.e., protecting your brothers while fighting for your country). Your faith, the wrong words at the wrong time, or your behaviors and actions – anything that doesn't line up with or match those of your fellow teammates – can put you on the wrong side of that club.

That was me.

Perhaps it was my faith that set me apart (I know for a fact it pissed off several of the guys). Or perhaps it was the severity of the hazing. Ultimately, the reason made no difference at all. But there I was, straddling a fence that kept me from gaining full acceptance into the brotherhood and it was difficult to maneuver.

Over the last couple of decades, the hazing of new recruits has received a lot of attention, but being that it all happens behind closed doors, there really is no way to police or monitor the activity. From the top-brass down, the theory is that hazing is only brought to light when it has gone too far.

By in large, the military has tried to reduce the amount of hazing, but it is still alive and well in the Teams.

But what you have to endure all depends on which task unit or platoon you land in. Some platoons are better than others and actually grasp the concept of mentoring, coaching and proper leadership. Others micromanage, intimidate and incorporate hazing as one of the "scare tactics" to keep you in line.

Unfortunately for me, I landed in a team that believed in the latter.

I had heard the horror stories (and eventually witnessed them first-hand) of guys being strapped to backboards with claymore clacker electrodes clipped to their nipples. Others had their heads shaved and a half of a milk carton glued to their heads, at which point they were dragged around the platoon quarters in an effort to humiliate them.

Fresh meat. That is the term of endearment for the new guys. I heard stories of various "beat down" sessions in which the platoon would turn off the lights and proceed to physically punish the new guys.

Some endured having their butt cracks, armpits or chests spray glued, or whatever other sadistic ideas the platoon leaders could come up with.

Hazing predominantly happened among the enlisted guys, while the officers would just chuckle and turn the other way.

Some of what the platoons put you through is considered tradition, and that was just fine. Others took it way too far.

My platoon was made up of way too many men who had not grown up yet. Perhaps they were still trying to prove to themselves that they were men. Or perhaps they were inclined to perpetuate the mistreatment by doing to us what was done to them.

I couldn't even begin to count the number of times that I was hit in the face or physically struck. I was made to carry a large 100-pound plank of wood across my back (my cross to bear) for miles, stared face down at the concrete while doing hundreds of pushups in temperatures in excess of 100 degrees, and ridiculed and mocked while going through my various "beatdown" sessions.

For me, one session included pulling tires in the Mississippi heat in mid-August for two hours straight. Much like my swimming days, I threw up so many times that I lost track. Another time, I sprinted up a steep, 800-foot hill until I passed out.

And in what felt like my own hostage situation, I was bound, blindfolded and brought to a military car wash station at which point a pillowcase was placed over my head and I was continuously sprayed with a power washer. The sheer pressure of the water burned my skin to that point that if felt like it would peel away from my body at any second.

I don't know what they hoped to gain by this modified "waterboarding" technique, but for me, it created nothing but anger, resentment and distrust in a group of people who were supposed to be my brothers or the men whose backs I was supposed to have on the missions to come.

"F**k-f**k" games. That's what they called them. And the new guys were often only left to guess what kind of torturous games they were going to be playing with us during the sets of training still to come.

The stress of it all was almost too much to bear. I so deeply wanted to avoid punishment that I would inevitably make even more mistakes.

The whole concept is so self-defeating and achieves the opposite results of what is really needed in an elite team of men. These childish games that many platoon leaders play serve no point other than for men to take their anger, aggression and hatred out on others. Many are probably recovering from their own "daddy issues."

And it's the reason why, in my second platoon, we took a different course of action – and treated our new batch of fresh meat with more respect. We saw the value in teaching and mentoring the new guys to become the best operators they could be, while building trust, camaraderie and respect among them.

I wish I could say there were more platoons like my second one – who focused on building up their teams rather than breaking them down – but that would be a lie. And unfortunately, what happens in the Teams, stays in the Teams.

Don't get me wrong. The SEAL Teams are amazing and life-changing. A lot of what they promote is good, healthy, honorable and admirable.

But in my experience, at the end of the day, it's less of a brotherhood and more of an "every guy for himself" environment. It's all about personal advancement in the Navy and doing whatever is needed to make yourself look good.

CHAPTER 3

Forged by Fire

Don't surrender your lifelong dreams to escape temporary pain.

I breathed a sigh of relief as Hell Week came to an end. I looked forward to smooth sailing from here on out.

Boy, was I wrong.

Truth be told, had I known how long it would actually take to become a SEAL, I probably would have made sure I was more mentally prepared for the long-haul.

At the time I went through the SEAL pipeline, BUD/S was several steps down the road. After completing my A-School as a parachute rigger, I loaded my beloved bride into my 2004 soft-top Jeep Wrangler and we made our cross-country trek from Pensacola, Florida to Coronado, California.

We gave ourselves a few more days of leeway because it was the only opportunity we had to honeymoon. We made the best of it as we drove the I-10 stretch, stopping at various places along the way. I think our stop in Louisiana and all the food we enjoyed along the way were my favorite parts. Hooyah, gumbo!

But once I showed up and checked in at the Coronado Amphibious Base, I knew it was time to get dialed in again. The honeymoon was over, and it was time to go to work.

We had to go through five weeks of Indoctrination (Indoc) before week one/day one of BUD/S. Indoc is a time of ramping up for what is physically and mentally to come – and all of Naval Special Warfare still goes through it.

There are two branches of Naval Special Warfare: SEALs and Special Warfare Combat Crewmen (SWCC). The SWCC guys are the ones that drive the Mark V boats which are loaded with .50 caliber machine guns, automatic grenade launchers (ALGLs) and twin 240s (two belt-fed .762 machine guns). (On a side note, these are the same three weapons systems that we had to mount on our HUMMVS overseas.)

We often joked that the SWCC guys were our water taxi cab drivers, but all kidding aside, they saved our asses more than once. They were truly solid and devoted men.

The SWCC candidates joined the SEALS with Indoc before moving on to their own training program which, as I understand it, is far different than BUD/S — and may explain the lower attrition rate of about 30% - 40%.

As Indoc wrapped up for me, I was thinking that the initial five weeks wasn't too bad, and I was prepared to sail smoothly into BUD/S. That was my first mistake.

I had no clue what was coming.

BUD/S is a six-month school where the boys truly become men. Every muscle, every fiber of your being is challenged. Stretched.

Forged.

Think about that word for one minute. *Forged.* "To form by heating and hammering; beat into shape."

But if you must know, getting through BUD/S is less about molding our bodies into the perfect physical specimen of a warrior, and far more a test and molding of mental capacity – let's call it 20% physical and 80% mental. Most people are surprised to hear me say that, because when they picture a BUD/S candidate, they are picturing the epitome of physical strength and agility.

The reality is, though, that the program is designed to *physically* break you in order to see how you cope *mentally*. Instructors look for that crucial moment when the body can no longer perform, to see how, in times of desperation and survival, you can command your body to perform beyond anything you could ever expect it to perform.

So, by far, mental toughness is one of the key characteristics all Team Guys possess.

BUD/S is divided into three phases of two months each.

The sole goal of the SEAL instructors in Phase 1 is to make you quit. In other words, life sucks. Really. There are no redeeming qualities for trainees going through the first phase other than to break us. This is where a majority of the attrition from the program happens – typically, the Team loses 80-90% of the trainees in that time.

Don't believe me?

My class – Class 253 - started with 221 guys. By the time training ended, there were all of 23 of the original guys left.

Now, if you've seen any movie related to SEAL training at all (ever), you've probably seen weary soldiers dragging their run-down bodies slowly and agonizingly toward a bell that they will ring three times to admit defeat. This is called "drop on request" or DOR.

But not everyone who leaves a class is considered a DOR. There are also three different ways a candidate can get "rolled" to the next class.

Performance Roll. A performance roll allows candidates to move on to the next class despite three failures of one of the weekly timed evolutions. These evolutions include a 2-mile swim, obstacle course or 4-mile run. The catch here is that this kind of roll is only granted if the instructor deems you a good guy and not a "turd."

Keep in mind though, "rollback land" isn't just a free pass for those who are rolled this way. It's merely a second chance. During this time, you are required to muster several times a day and work on your deficiencies.

The SEAL instructors in rollback land are a little more lenient, but they will still hammer you if you piss them off.

Medical Roll. A medical roll is as obvious as it sounds. You get hurt and can't physically keep going. Again, the instructors gather and determine if they want to send you back to the fleet or medically roll you to the next class. Now, the good news about medical roll is that it can be a welcome break while you have time to recover.

Shin splints which turn to stress fractures. Broken bones. Concussions. Pneumonia. Random serious illnesses. These are all reasons why people may get medically rolled. In my case, the closest I came to a medical roll was when I ended up with cellulitis in my elbow after Hell Week. If you think that sounds gross, it is.

It took something as small as a granule of sand poking a small hole in my skin, followed by rolling around in less than clean water to create five long pockets of pus running from my elbow to my mid-forearm. I remember doctors cutting it open and squeezing out the oozy pus. I recall the cautious whispers of the doctors saying they had never seen such a bad case before.

Further testing on the infection revealed that it was highly contagious, so I was not allowed to be around the elderly, children or anyone with a compromised immune system. Still, no medical roll for me on that one. Thank God.

But, given the timing of Danielle's cancer diagnosis which was just after my completion of the first phase, I ended up in the third type of roll – the admin roll.

Admin Roll. This overarching term was for any roll that is neither medical- nor performance-related. So, for example, if a family emergency or unforeseen tragedy occurred, the instructors could grant an admin roll that would allow the student to drop out of one class and continue with the next class.

"Koontz!" yelled the instructor.

I was paralyzed. If you ever had the occasion to be called down to the principal's office in school, you are well-familiar with that feeling. Only imagine that feeling times ten. My mind quickly scrolled through everything and anything I had done to put me in this position.

But I wasn't in trouble after all. And amazingly, it was the first time I ever remember looking at my instructors as peers.

They sat me down and looked me in the eye for what was about to be a challenging heart-to-heart.

The instructors had heard the news of Danielle's diagnosis and wanted to talk to me about my options.

"We understand the situation and will not hold you at fault for stepping away from training," they said. "We can station you in a location so you can fully support Danielle and what she's going through."

My mind was made up. "I'm staying."

Danni and I had already discussed my choice and career path many times. She was so amazing, and completely supportive of fulfilling my dream to stay in BUD/S.

The instructors were equally supportive, saying they would do whatever they could to make sure I had time with her, especially during her appointments.

Honestly though, to say that going through it was difficult is an understatement. It was like calling a mental time out in the final seconds of a tied game in playoffs. I was torn and distracted and couldn't let anyone know about it.

If Danielle knew how much I was going through, it wouldn't have been fair to her. And I wouldn't have been the best, most supportive husband I needed to be during daily radiation treatments, chemo treatments, surgeries and other hospital visits. Balboa Hospital was turning into a second home.

If I brought my problems into BUD/S, I couldn't perform at my best and prove myself to be the warrior I was meant to be. But the reality was, I was distracted and it was affecting my performance.

It was then that I had a crash-course in strengthening my ability to compartmentalize. I've always done it well, but I needed to do it better.

It was like living in two different worlds. A dichotomy. And I was straddling the fence the best I could.

In one world, I was a supportive, loving, tender, compassionate husband at the hospital and in the other world, and a tough, strong determined warrior in training.

I remember having shouting matches with God, followed by quiet moments of tears as I asked what the hell was going on with my life and why God would allow something so horrible to happen. But I also knew He was big enough to handle my questions and accusations.

I spent about two months in rollback land, during which time I joined Danielle at important hospital visits while maintaining my rigorous physical routine. I remember running, swimming and doing physical training quite a bit during those times. Sometimes, I look back at those times and wonder how in the world I ever made it through the most emotionally trying time of my life.

I have to give God credit for keeping me sane.

And Danielle, of course. She was my greatest fan.

I know for a fact that she played a pivotal role in my training. Despite feeling depleted and exhausted every night when I came home, Danielle would eagerly greet me and listen as I regaled her with the stories of my day. There wasn't a night that she didn't rub my feet until I passed out. She would hang out with the boys on the weekends while we played Texas Hold'em, smoked cigars and helped out however she could. She was so, so loving, and it still brings tears to my eyes that I was so blessed to have her in my life. To this day, I swear I can feel and picture her smiling down on me.

Before I shipped out to boot camp, Danielle would travel with me to various events in the Northeast – whether it was my screen test, or a small group of soon-to-be-BUD/S candidates who would spend a weekend together training at the Jersey Shore.

Boot camp was no different. I would sneak away to call her just so she could hear my voice and know I was okay. I could see her smile through the phone every time she laughed. It – no, she – was amazing. Her ear-to-ear grin and adorable laugh graced the room at my graduation from both boot camp and BUD/S.

So, coming full circle, I started BUD/S and completed first phase with Class 253 and finished phases two and three with Class 254.

> *Positivity is not the question of denying reality or wearing rose-colored glasses. It is in the mindset of accepting reality and knowing that this too shall pass.*

The infamous "Hell Week" usually falls between the fourth and fifth week of the first phase. This is where candidates are forced to stay awake for five days straight.

Actually, that's not true.

On days four and five, we get the privilege of sleeping for one hour each day. It's worse, I think, to have those hours. A tease to both the body and the mind.

I'm pretty sure that medically a person is diagnosed as insane if they go more than three consecutive days without sleep – so technically, I may be insane.

I remember very, very little about Hell Week. It was cold. Dark. Wet. Other than that, my memory of that week is pretty much a cold, dark, wet void.

I do, however, distinctly remember two stories.

Surf torture. Day two.

You have likely seen this surf torture portrayed in the movies as well. During surf torture, the instructors send the students into the ocean where they lay down and lock arms with one another. The students' bodies and heads are repeatedly bashed by the waves.

The purpose of this exercise is to push the body to the point of hypothermia and beyond to see how you will react. Medical personnel are on-hand to chart the water temperature and monitor our vital signs — ultimately, they are charting how long the human body can sustain that water temperature before hypothermia sets.

Given the severity of our training, it wasn't uncommon to see a white truck (normally a F-350) called the "ambu" or ambulance standing by on every evolution.

The ambu pulled up as it always did, and out stepped the Instructor Echaloga. Towering over us at 6'4", this Latino instructor barking through a bullhorn couldn't be missed.

"Ladies! The nighttime is the right time!" was the nightly phrase he'd howl over and over in an attempt to persuade us to quit.

But somehow this night was different.

I looked over at the truck and noticed what appeared to be steam wafting out of the bed of the truck.

Hallucinations, for sure, I thought.

But the steam was real. Fresh, hot steam coming from a hot tub the instructors had filled up in the bed of the truck. And it didn't end there. The instructors had also purchased six dozen fresh, piping hot Crispy Crème donuts.

Instructor Echaloga came back on the bullhorn.

"The nighttime is the right time! Listen up! The first six students to touch the ambu and quit get to sit in this hot tub as long as they want AND eat a dozen Crispy Crème donuts!"

No sooner had the words left his mouth, multiple students jumped out of the surf and made a mad dash for the truck.

I remember thinking, "I know we're miserable right now, but is your SEAL career really worth a hot bath and a donut? I mean, those donuts are good – but are they THAT good?"

The second story I remember occurred as I was about to embark upon the longest evolution of BUD/S during Hell Week called the around-the-world tour. This evolution is a series of tasks covering about 85 miles around the San Diego/Coronado Bay that starts after the second day of no sleep and takes about a day-and-a-half to complete. During this time, we are in a non-stop cycle of either running through the soft sand on the beach carrying our boats on top of our heads or we'd be rowing our "inflatable boats small" (IBS) through the water.

And I remind you. No sleep.

So, you can imagine both the hysteria and hysterics that ensue.

Sometimes, guys would fall asleep while paddling only to be shocked awake by the cold ocean water smacking against their bodies when they had fallen out. They'd promptly wake up and jump right back into the boats.

For me, I remember paddling and paddling and paddling and suddenly looking out at the water and seeing hundreds of Snickers bars floating by. I was hungry and clearly delirious. And I mean, "You're not you when you're hungry." Or so the commercials say anyway.

While I'm still amused by the thought of rowing through a sea of those brown-wrapped candy bars, the rest of this story is a bit more sobering.

This particular evolution started in the middle of the night. My boat crew was given the green light to begin and we began running down the beach. We hadn't even made it a hundred yards when —

SNAP!

The pain in my leg was excruciating. It radiated throughout my whole body and I instantly hit the ground.

My whole SEAL career flashed before my eyes. I didn't want to be medically rolled. I didn't want to fail.

I said the quickest and only prayer I could think of at that moment. "God help me."

And He answered.

I found the strength to pull my body out of the sand, limped my way back to my waiting crew and continued through the rest of Hell Week with minimal pain and discomfort.

Once Hell Week is secured on Friday afternoon, we went through medical checks. That sound on the beach that day that brought me to my knees? That was the sound of my IT band tearing.

Luckily, the week after Hell Week is "Walk Week" in which we wear tennis shoes and walk everywhere instead of run. It gave us time to recuperate.

The second phase of BUD/S is the dive phase, which is equally as demanding physically as the first phase. During this time, we learn how to SCUBA dive on open-circuit systems (which emit bubbles when you breathe) and closed-circuit systems called Dragers. A Drager is a rebreather that is used for more clandestine missions because they don't emit bubbles – which means they don't give away our position.

The Drager system uses pure oxygen, a breathing bag and Sofnolime to convert the CO_2 that we exhale into the O_2 that we inhale. With the Drager system, the oxygen bottle only lasts up to four hours.

The instructors in this phase, just like the earlier phase, often give students "beatdown" sessions.

In one beatdown session, we all had to cram into a small room and, as a class, do 500 8-count bodybuilders – think of a burpee, but far more evil. When it was all over, I remember looking at the walls and see condensation from our own steam and sweat covering the walls.

Second phase had two very challenging and mandatory tests.

First, the two-minute tread.

I know what you're thinking. "Easy! You have fins on!"

But we're wearing 60-pound air tanks on our backs. And can't use our arms.

Believe it or not, many students fail this evolution and are performance rolled into the next class.

The second evolution, which takes place in the last week of the second phase, is called pool comp and puts all of your diving skills to the test.

Instructors would rip the mouth pieces from students, tie the air hoses in knots, and slam us around on the bottom of the pool to simulate a surf hit. These hits sent our bodies flailing about like rag dolls.

The goal and the expectation are that we remain calm. Composed. And that we fix the problem. Hoses get untied. Tanks get put back on. Gear gets situated.

All in one breath.

Those who panic and bolt to the surface fail the evolution.

The third and final phase is a combination of weapons training, land navigation and mock missions (also called Field Training Exercises or FTXs). This two-month stretch is divided up into two locations in California, Coronado and San Clemente Island. It is in this phase when most students will handle their secondary weapons (SIG226) and their primary weapons (M4) for the first time. We also get exposed to automatic weapons like the M46 and M48, also called the SAW or Sub Automatic Machine guns which fire the .556 and .762 rounds. We're also exposed to C4, the main explosives used in the Teams.

Blowing stuff up sounds easy, I know.

Make no mistake though, this phase is quite possibly even more physically challenging than the previous two phases. But by this time, the brothers who are by your side are more likely than not the brothers who won't quit and will finish BUD/S with you. The worst was doing "pallet runs" up Frog Hill. This 200-yard/40- degree incline hill became our daily reminder how much dedication it took to stick it out until the end. We had to run it multiple times a day. And when you screwed up, you got to trade in your wood pallet for a metal one. Fun times.

The third phase also consists of a five-mile open swim off the shore of San Clemente Island – which conveniently happens to be a very popular breeding ground for great white sharks.

So, what did the instructors do to "motivate" us?

Showed us movie clips of *Jaws*, of course.

And ...

In preparation, the instructors lined us up on the grinder (a fancy word for a large slab of concrete) and had us lay down like packed sardines. It wasn't long before I noticed two large buckets to the left and the right of us. And slowly, but surely, those instructors approached from either side dumping the contents of the buckets over us.

Fish chum.

The warm, blood, guts, bones, and carcasses of fish slathered over our bodies made us tasty treats for the sharks whose homes we were about to swim directly through. Awesome.

But here I am living to tell the story as a 2005 BUD/S graduate, Class 254.

Following graduation, we were off to the Army base in Fort Benning, Georgia for static line jump school.

Fortunately (or unfortunately as it turns out), the next step in the process was nothing like the agonizing adventures of my BUD/S days. Actually, if I'm being honest, it was the most mind-numbing month of my life. Worse than my plain white cubicle days? No, probably not, but boring no less.

Now, with temperatures in the upper 90's and low 100's, Georgia in August is nothing short of unpleasant. The instructors paid no mind to the heat and insisted we practice our Parachute Landing Falls (PLFs) on top of 1' by 1' boxes in an open field for hours upon hours. Without exaggeration, I was drinking 12 canteens of water a day and still pissing orange.

Miserable is an understatement.

The only saving grace for us Navy guys is that we could stay off base if wanted to. We're no dummies. We all opted to stay at an extended-stay motel for the month instead of the run-down, World War II, lead-infested barracks on base.

With the PLF training complete, we moved on to planes for the real deal.

Sure, we were jumping out of planes, but in static line jumping, the ripcord is attached to a cable in the aircraft that automatically deploys the parachute as the single-file line of jumpers leave the aircraft. The point of the static line is to ensure that every jumper is under canopy in the air at the same time.

The catch here is that the Army jump school is still using old T-10 parachutes without ventilation holes, steering or flaring capabilities, so you're really at the mercy of the wind that day. We'd often end up as human lawn darts, hitting the ground so hard that you'd have the wind knocked right out of you. I often felt like my spine was an accordion.

I can thank the Army for the herniated S2 disk in my back.

These days, the Navy has taken static line jump school out of the pipeline – a decision that really seemed like a no-brainer to me. Now, the students head straight to Arizona for freefall jump school to practice High Altitude High Opening (HAHO) and High Altitude Low Opening (HALO) jumps. When all is said and done, I'd say this is a better use of time and government resources because Team guys won't ever go on a mission where they are required to take a static jump.

Once Free Fall school is completed, the students head back to Coronado for another six months of training, called SEAL Qualification Training (SQT). Unlike the "fresh meat" treatment candidates received in BUD/S, the instructors are more like mentors and coaches in this phase.

SQT is a time for us to fine-tune our skills before landing on a SEAL team. Here, we'd perfect our diving, land navigation, weapons qualifications, become introduced to our Zodiaks (our 14' rubber boats), etc.

Speaking of SQT and Zodiaks. One sunny afternoon in the San Diego Bay area, we were driving around in our boats, enjoying the training. Well, some of us got a little too carried away. There were at least a half a dozen Zodiaks out there tooling around and none of us had any clue what we were doing. At the time, I was riding in the middle of my Zodiak when suddenly another Zodiak turned and T-boned us.

Apparently, the driver didn't see us, but they were driving so fast that their Zodiak actually hit ours and flew over! I remember it hitting my head and temporarily knocking me out. To this day, I don't know how the prop of the 55hp engine didn't split my head in two.

Anyway, I digress. SQT is the light at the end of the tunnel – the last phase before being awarded our Tridents.

The trident is the SEAL's military insignia, or as we like to call it, our "Budweiser" or "Bird." This military insignia includes four components that are symbolic of everything that is SEAL – Sea, Air and Land.

There are two elements to represent the sea: Poseidon's pitchfork (the trident) and the anchor. There is one image to represent land – musket – and finally, the bald eagle to represent air.

Interestingly, the portrayal of the eagle on our Trident is the only time you will see the American bald eagle represented with its head bowed to show respect for the fallen brothers who have gone before us.

Following the pinning ceremony, the proud class makes its way to a particular bar to celebrate what is likely to be the biggest accomplishments of their lives.

There's drinking. Man, is there drinking. Which goes right along with a rite of passage for graduates. And I'll tell you, it's not for the squeamish.

The newly pinned graduates take off their shirts and place the Tridents on our chests where the insignia would be affixed to our uniforms. One by one, we make that badge a physical part of us as we take turns punching the three half-inch spikes of the pin into our classmates' flesh. It sounds terrible, but between the pride and the alcohol, we couldn't feel a thing.

But even with all this celebration, it was still only the beginning of the journey.

At this point, the government allows each SEAL to pick the coast where they would like to be stationed. When it came time for me to choose, Danielle was still fighting the battle of her life with breast cancer, so together we decided to choose the East Coast because the housing market was a bit more favorable and we had heard the healthcare at Portsmouth Hospital was stellar.

We took a life-changing trip across the country, landing in Little Creek, Virginia where we purchased our first home together less than two miles away from the Amphibious Base. Our home, a modest 1,200 square foot abode, was nothing to brag about, but it was our sanctuary. We stayed there for a year and then decided it would be best for Danielle to move back home to Yakima, Washington where her family and a state-of-the-art cancer center called North Star Lodge was located.

The Naval Special Warfare Command decided to station me on SEAL Team 10. That may sound familiar to you if you have seen the movie *Lone Survivor* or read Marcus Luttrell's book. Team 10 was the 18-member Quick Reaction Force (QRF) on board the Chinook that was shot down with a rocket propelled grenade (RPG) while trying to get Marcus Luttrell's team out of harm's way on June 28, 2005.

Showing up to a team that had just suffered a tragic loss of life was sobering to say the least, as I was stepping directly into the shoes of one of our fallen brothers.

I was faced with the very heavy reality that my profession, forged by fire, could possibly come with the greatest cost: my life.

But I was ready to pay that price – for the sake of my country and my loved ones.

CHAPTER 4

The Treacherous Path

You can only endeavor to surround yourself with good people who know and support you. Be intentional about building those relationships.

The path of a new guy is a treacherous and arduous path indeed.

Not only are there many new skills to learn and combat scenarios to navigate, but adjusting to the culture of the SEAL teams is nearly as challenging.

Each of the nine different teams share the same general culture – Type A guys who are hard-charging, loud and aggressive. But each task unit and platoon has their own unique aspects of culture that are mixed in with the larger SEAL pot.

Let's just say that as a new guy, you get pretty used to drinking out of the firehose.

New guys must learn the new details and intricacies of all the departments such as diving, air, engineering and armory, to name a few, but they also have to understand the temperaments and personalities of the roughly 15 other men with whom they will be spending the majority of their lives.

Top all of that off with having the pressure of making sound tactical decisions in trainings (which, many times, are live-fire evolutions) and in war. That's not an easy feat.

These guys are intense both on the field and off, meaning during training and after hours.

There are a few phrases that echo off the halls of every team that many SEALs either consciously or subconsciously live by: "Work hard, play harder" and "Go big or go home."

So, when the work is done, it's time to play harder and go big.

Those who don't drink (which, by the way, is generally respected in the Teams) can show up and drink Coke all night, and those who don't go to the strip clubs can hang out in the government vans until everyone is ready to leave.

Translation: Most new guys find themselves taking turns playing chauffeur for the rest of the platoon.

These large white government vans are anything but inconspicuous driving around town, especially when you consider the wars that go on inside them.

Yes, wars – van wars.

Often times, a simple nod from a senior enlisted signals an all-out fight inside these large vehicles. No man is exempt from the brawling. Not even the driver.

By the time the doors open, every man who files (or falls) out, has a cut, a bloody nose, or some other wound. The seats are often ripped or broken. The windows are splattered with blood. Clothes are torn. And the smell of testosterone, sweat, and camaraderie prevails.

Sure, we'd get yelled at or scolded, but the moments of hysteria and chaos were always well worth the punishments.

But I digress.

As fun as these times were, it was often challenging to balance the moral compass among Team guys, especially for men of faith like me.

Sticking to my morals was probably the finest of lines I have ever had to walk. And I admit, I did not walk that line very well.

Let me ask you a question.

How do you gain the respect and trust of your brothers – the very same brothers you would take a bullet for in combat – without participating in their "extracurricular" activities or even talking the talk? After all, I wasn't someone who took to swearing, dirty jokes or degrading women.

I wanted them to accept me though – perhaps that was my insecure formative years coming back to haunt me. I wanted them to like me. To respect me. But without having to do the same things they were doing.

This rarely jives in the wolf pack.

If you find yourself on the outside because you look or act different, you will spend the rest of your time as a new guy fighting an inward battle or tug-of-war. On the one side, you want to fit into the brotherhood, while on the other one, you want to stay true to your beliefs.

My deep desire to blend led me down some very dark paths in the Navy. And sometimes – even now, as I look out the foggy window of my plane – I wonder what decisions I would make differently if given the chance to do it all over again.

Over and over, I compromised my identity and beliefs just to be one of the guys. These compromises, some big, some small, ultimately led some of them to judge me, disrespect me, and write me off.

I can't blame them, really, even though I think it was unfair and unwarranted.

There were times, for example, that I choose to partake in far too many alcoholic beverages. That choice never resulted in anything good, but in my mind, I felt that the more I acted like my brothers, the more likely they would accept me.

My language became crude, vulgar.

And eventually, I ended up getting romantically involved with a woman besides my wife.

I am not making excuses. I made those choices. I own them. And they were wrong.

When you're in it – I mean, deep in it – you just never realize how the people we choose to hang out with influence our behavior. I often tell parents, "You show me your kids' friends and I'll show you their future."

Most of us can choose our friends and those we hang out with, but in SEAL teams, we are not afforded those choices. We are thrown into a mixing pot and have to make the best of it.

Maybe someone like you could handle that kind of pressure – and I hope you always can. But we're all fooling ourselves if we say that we don't feel that strong pull to act, think and behave like those we are surrounded by.

And for those of you who, at the very reading of these words, are reliving the detrimental mistakes you've made in the past, it's NEVER too late to start fresh and anew. I believe in second, third, fourth, and fifth chances – so please don't ever think you have reached the point of no return or are beyond help.

After my experiences in the Teams, I always told myself that I would do my best to paint a clear picture for young men who wanted to enter the program. My intent or motive now is not in any way, shape, or form to discourage anyone from joining. It's simply to let them know the truth behind *my* Trident.

This daily life that often goes overlooked, unexplored, and unacknowledged needs to be known by these young men so they can know what they are getting themselves into and make educated decisions along the way.

Without a doubt, good leadership can really ease this time of transition. But there are leaders and there are managers.

Leaders put others first. They lead by example and appropriately challenge and encourage those they lead. They empower those they are responsible for, give feedback on areas for improvement and strengthen their team by emphasizing positive values, beliefs, actions and words.

Managers, on the other hand, tell people what to do. They bark orders, micromanage their subordinates and tend to be verbally aggressive, dominant and abrasive.

There is a world of difference between these two leadership styles. And when you're America's elite training for the most dangerous environments and missions, this gap in leadership style is exacerbated.

In my first platoon, I was immersed in the management leadership style which created a stressful internal struggle.

You see, I'm the type of person who doesn't thrive under someone's thumb. I can't breathe. I feel stifled to the point that I hesitate and make mistakes. And in this field, you simply can't make mistakes, because mistakes can cost you your life or worse -- the life of your brothers.

As a new guy, the more I focused my emotional energy on not screwing up, the more I messed up. The more I would get hammered, punished for my mistakes.

How was this even helpful? It only fueled the vicious cycle of rage pumping through my veins.

It wasn't just me. I have personally witnessed young, very impressionable new guys who were "managed" developing a certain fear or hesitancy while those who are coached, mentored and truly lead end up having a confidence, assurance and stability in their platoon that carries over onto the battlefield.

So how can you tell what kind of leadership style you will fall under when you first show up to your team? Honestly, you can't.

My best advice is to look at the professionalism and maturity of the Platoon Chief and the "upper head-shed" to get an idea of the leadership culture that is forming. It is crazy to think about but virtually every SEAL platoon has its own unique culture. Each one is lead and systematically organized differently. Each platoon also has its own unique way of internally relating to one another.

The top leadership is either empowering and pulls people up to their level, or they are insecure and use others to boost themselves up.

And typically, those who used their position to boost themselves up, often did so through controlling, aggressive and dominant behavior.

Truly, I don't think these types of leaders even see the harm and dysfunction in their words and actions. Deep down, I think they are so insecure about their identity that they subconsciously believe that the only way they'll garner respect is to belittle and demean the guys in their platoon.

Many of the "One Platoon Wonders" operated in this way during my first pump (or 2-year cycle). These "One Platoon Wonders" are men who have just one deployment under their belts and are then handed the great power and responsibility to train the incoming new guys. They are typically unaware that there is any other way to lead and therefore end up perpetuating the same damaging practices inflicted upon them when they were new guys.

We called our Platoon Chief "SAM" for "Short Angry Man." He ruled with an iron fist, lost his temper at a whim, and got flustered by the smallest things. Most of us just rolled our eyes and ignored him, however, his leadership style, personality, and negativity were contagious. When all five of us new guys showed up to our platoon, we knew (based on reputation and gossip) that we were stepping into a field full of land mines.

Still, solid life lessons can be learned even under poor leadership. As a matter of fact, many times people learn how to do the right things by observing first-hand from others how not to do them. For example, I learned that micromanaging is incredibly stifling and restricts those people you are trying to lead.

Instead of instilling confidence and empowering the people they are training, the micromanager's own fear and insecurity drives that leader to put others under their thumb. They may not even know that they are coming across as controlling and dominant, but ultimately, they are producing individuals who either leave the organization entirely or become resentful and unfulfilled. And by doing so, an individual's potential is wasted and unused, causing the culture of the organization to suffer.

Another lesson learned merely by observing the wrong way to lead a team is the system of punishment versus reward.

The punishment system scolds others for the wrong behavior or making a simple mistake. The rewards system, on the other hand, recognizes – even praises – good behavior and solid decisions. And the rewards system always wins because the focus is on what's right, rather than what's wrong. This is an excellent parenting technique (and one that I try to implement) as well as an excellent way to achieve the positive results from those you lead.

Picture the age-old image of a lone tree in a large field with a car smashed into it. You can't help but think, 'How in the hell did that driver manage to crash into the only tree in the field?"

Simply put, that lone tree was all the driver could see through the window of the out-of-control car. The driver had such tunnel vision that the intense concentration not to hit the tree, caused the driver to hit the one thing he was trying to avoid.

In other words, what we choose to focus on has a direct impact on the end result.

Take my training, for example. I was so fearful of making mistakes that I either didn't take calculated chances or react in a timely manner – or simply screwed up. And was punished for it as a result. On the teams, we called this "paying the man."

I hated paying the man and being reprimanded for my mistakes because it ultimately ended up reinforcing the exact behavior I was trying to avoid.

Yes, my first platoon was hard — no ifs, ands, or buts about it. But the life lessons I learned throughout those challenging two years were priceless and I am grateful to have had them.

Without those trials and tribulations, I would never have gained the valuable insights into human behavior nor formed the characteristics that make me who I am today.

Both Sides of the Same Coin

I have looked pure evil in the face and stared back with God-like vengeance.

Being a breacher is one of the main jobs on the SEAL teams. Other jobs are medic (or a corpsman), communications and sniper.

As I said earlier, breachers like to blow things up. It's as fun as it sounds, but certainly isn't all we do.

We have other tools at our disposal for whatever situations we find ourselves in. For example, when overseas, we primarily used bolt cutters for clandestine missions on gates and fences. We also used sledge hammers with seven-pound heads and collapsible stocks. Other times, when faced with high walls, like in the Osama bin Laden raid, we would carry collapsible ladders.

Hullie tools allowed us to smash through windows when the element of surprise wasn't in order and we had to gain entry as quickly as possible. And more – quickie saws for metal doors and iron bars, torches that burned at 10,000 degrees Fahrenheit for solid steel ship doors and hatches, chainsaws for wood doors and fences, shotguns for door hinges and deadbolt locks. Lock pick sets for the super-sneaky-peaky missions and "slap charges," a roughly 1' by 2" datasheet which has a C4 explosive composite, used mainly overseas. The charge had an adhesive on one side, so we literally ran up to the door, peeled the backing off the charge and "slapped" it on the door at the perfect spot so the charge, when detonated, would literally slice through the door — opening it upon detonation.

My job as a Lead Breacher, simply put, was to get our boys on the X as quickly and safely as possible. I had to be prepared for everything and anything the party called for.

Take the Osama bin Laden raid, for example. His compound was surrounded by walls made of reinforced concrete that was close to three-feet thick. Knowing this ahead of time, they could have constructed an explosive charge called a "shape charge" which had the ability to simultaneously blow and slice through a very large target. Instead, due to the nature of the mission, they clandestinely climbed over the walls with collapsible ladders.

The bigger/thicker the obstacle, the bigger the charge.

We had to be careful though, because nothing ruins the element of surprise like an explosive that wasn't big enough to get the job done. Nothing could be more dangerous and put your fireteam in harm's way than ruining the element of surprise (and simultaneously not gaining entry).

Now, the flip side of this is that you can't have too large of a charge either, because you have to protect your brothers and keep their melons from being concussed. And bringing a house down due to a larger explosion also defeats the purpose.

Needless to say, building explosives requires careful planning and complex calculations to do it right. We use PETN – the explosive component found in C4 – as our baseline. PETN's explosive composition is 1.66 (with TNT being the baseline of 1.0). The safe standoff distance is calculated by this number as well.

No pressure.

Actually, that reminds me of the final day of Breacher School. For our final test, the instructors had built a barricade behind a door located at the top of a stairwell. The stairwell consisted of a single flight of about twenty stairs and was about 12 to 18 inches wide with walls on either side. The door was barricaded so well that halfway through we had to get the chainsaw out.

So, there I was, my back against the wall and my legs braced against the other wall. I had to change the blade three times before I was able to get through the portion of the door that was barricaded. At one point, I had to pull out the quickie saw as well because they put a steel beam across the door on the other side! The stairwell was sweltering. No air flow.

I grew lightheaded and dizzy. And all I could think was, "If I fall at this point, I'm a goner. I'm going to decapitate myself – or someone else."

Well, we finally got through that door with everybody still intact. The instructors had put so many two-by-fours and steel bars as barricades to really put us to the test.

But we did it. It was a good day and a good evolution of training.

One of the main reasons I'm writing this book is to shed light on the real life of a Navy SEAL; therefore, I would be remiss if I also didn't mention the effects of war and the challenges they can bring while transitioning into civilian life, even years or decades after being discharged.

General Douglas MacArthur depicts this best: "The soldier, above all other people, prays for peace for he must suffer and bear the deepest wounds and scars of war."

Our wounds and scars are real. And, hopefully our wounds become scars. Unfortunately, this is not the case for every service man or woman who is discharged from the military.

Over the last decade, there has been much research and progress in helping veterans deal with these wounds. I would like to think that Post Traumatic Stress Disorder (PTSD) is becoming less of a label or negative stigma and more of an accepted reality. I am grateful to the mental health professionals who have helped thousands of men and women that tread on an oftentimes lonely path.

I recently heard a statistic that twenty-two veterans a day take their own lives. **Twenty-two a day**. That's one every 65 minutes. Tragic.

This doesn't happen accidentally. It's a desperate cry to be seen, heard, and understood.

Even now, my eyes are welling up as I think about the personal effects of war that I have felt and seen happen to so many of my brothers.

Okay, let's go a bit deeper and more personal.

So many people, especially those in the special forces community, just want someone who can speak their language and relate to their experiences.

The power of presence is huge.

Just having someone to talk with and listen goes a very, very long way. Many feel isolated, unseen, and alone.

The guys whom I've met (and continue to meet with), only want to experience a bit of camaraderie to know that what they are feeling is normal.

Take me, for example. I had built up some pretty high walls – and then barricaded myself in so well that not even the best Lead Breacher could break through. I rarely let anyone inside those places of vulnerability and darkness.

I don't trust easily – and those areas are mainly reserved for me and God.

Every single operator I know struggles daily with the intense need to get back in the fight. We want to continually "see action." This is the internal tug-of-war that I mentioned earlier – the one that all of us warriors will have to live with for the rest of our lives.

This reminds me of a line in the movie *13 Hours* that hits me deep:

> Jack: Every time I go home to my family I think *this is it. I'm gonna stay*. Then something happens, and I end up back here (downrange). Why is that? Why can't I go home? Why can't I go home and just stay there?
>
> Glen: Warriors aren't trained to retire, Jack.

No matter how high I built my walls though, there were times when those closed-up emotions would come bounding over. For me, the emotional tiger leapt over that wall three years after my honorable discharge in late 2009 and revealed itself as intense anger. It was as if my body was trying to purge something.

Growing up in my teen years, I often felt like a caged animal – mostly because I wasn't given much of a voice with my strict mom and stepdad. I am sure this contributed, and in some ways helped, channel that aggression in the Teams.

Ironically, my first platoon's motto was "Victory Through Violence." As SEALs, we are taught to instantaneously assess the situation and apply the appropriate amount of force necessary in order to neutralize our threats before a dramatic back-off to continue assessing the situation and the scene. This allowed us to make strategically sound and tactical decisions. Sometimes that force is a fierce volley of fire or violent lethal action.

Whatever the case, we are taught and trained to regain and maintain control of very chaotic situations.

Most Team guys listen to heavy music all the time — while working out, prepping their gear, walking around the Team's building and even during some of our evolutions. Even now, while I'm sitting on the plane, I turned on a bit of Godsmack, Ramstein, and Demon Hunter to write this section of the book.

I can step into this world of aggression and anger instantly. It's not an out-of-control anger, but a very controlled aggression. If I'm being honest, sometimes it sneaks up and surprises me because it's powerful. I have learned in the past how to channel this and subdue it in a healthy way.

I kinda look at myself as a finely-tuned weapon with a hairpin trigger. And I've been able to manage the angry outbursts that come along with it through anger management counseling and continued self-awareness. But trust me, it's lurking there not too far beneath the surface.

Sometimes I feel like it wouldn't take much to push me over the edge, so it is a good thing that my personality helps me balance some of this out.

Like I've mentioned, I'm not your typical Type A personality. I can exhibit those traits, sure, but I tend to be more of a fun-loving guy who likes to tease and joke around. Some even say I'm a teddy bear.

I do, however, have to be aware of the things that trigger me and resist the tendency to go over to the "dark side" and let circumstances dictate my emotions.

If we are being honest, we all have a "dark side."

I like the analogy that we all sit on a figurative fence in life and on either side of that fence lives a dog – a "good" dog on one side and a "bad" dog on the other. We are consistently feeding either dog by the actions and choices we make. Eventually, one of those dogs is going to get big enough and strong enough to jump the fence and attack the other dog.

So, let me pose a question to you: *Which dog have you been feeding more lately?*

I have had to catch myself at times feeding the wrong dog. With each "right" choice we make, we starve the bad dog.

Again, in the interest of honesty, sometimes it feels good to feed the bad dog. I don't know why. Maybe it's just scratching that itch inside of me that will always be there. I can't dwell on these thoughts for too long or I will get lost in them. Once I recognize that my mind is wandering, I mostly distract myself by thinking of something different or even saying a prayer of sorts.

The thing that calms and quiets my mind the most is the gentle touch and affection of a woman. Every human has an innate desire to be seen, valued and loved, but for me, there's just something about the compassionate love of a woman that is a soothing balm on that anger and aggression.

Other guys I know have more self-destructive means of coping – adrenaline-producing activities, drugs and/or alcohol, women, or medication.

Honestly, I don't judge it. How could I?

You do what you have to do to get through it. Trust me, my liver has seen its fair share of action. Some of what we have been through and seen is horrific.

I have looked pure evil in the face and stared back with God-like vengeance. I have taken it by the throat and choked the life of it.

And I would do it again in a heartbeat. Hooyah!

CHAPTER 6

The Broad and Narrow Paths

Life and its challenges are simply what we make of them. Our perspective while encountering hardships determines what kind of filter we develop.

At the beginning of the book, I spoke about my Go Bag and the role it played in ensuring that we as SEALs were always prepared for whatever came our way. But remember, it's not just the physical tools that allowed us to succeed, but the mental tools that we packed as well.

In some cases, in fact, the mental tools were more crucial to succeeding in a mission.

As SEALs, we basically had to be prepared for four different types of missions, each requiring their own physical and mental preparation:

Surveillance and Reconnaissance (S&R). Typically, during S&R, four operators are inserted several "clicks" (or kilometers) away from the target where they set up a hide site and gather as much intelligence as possible.

The operators take pictures and videos and drawings of various details about the target. They'll note key terrain features, civil considerations, enemy movement, number of potential hostiles and building schematics, to name a few. Every possible detail you can imagine was documented in order to ready the team as best as possible.

The most famous S&R mission was phase one of Operation Red Wings in which Marcus Latrell, Danny Dietz, Lt. Michael Murphey and Matthew G. Axelson were sent out to basically gather intelligence on the potential safe house of Ahmad Shah. On the evening of June 27, 2005, Latrell and his fire team were inserted via fast-rope in the Pech District of Afghanistan's Kunar Province, on the side of a mountain named Sawtalo Sar, roughly 20 miles west of Kunar's provincial capital of Asadabad.

Unfortunately, their communication was subpar and had to move their position to get a better line of sight.

Once they finally bedded down, it was only a matter of time until they were discovered by goat herders who would create the biggest dilemma they would ever encounter.

See, according to the Geneva Convention and our standard operating procedures, we are not to engage the enemy (shoot them) if we don't perceive them as threats.

The goat herders were obviously no real threat, so ethically there was no justification for killing them. They were faced with two options: tie them up or let them go.

But the terrain and geography in Afghanistan is such that if they did zip-tie them to a tree, it would be days before they were found. And by that time, they would have either been attacked by animals or died of dehydration. So, realistically, they only one moral option that wouldn't make them culpable for the deaths of these shepherds.

Once they let the goat herders go, the youngest male made his way to the compound below and revealed the fire team's location. At that point, it was only a matter of time before a firefight erupted.

As the four-man team worked their way down the side of the mountain, all the while engaging the sizeable enemy force, they sustained injuries that would eventually claim the lives of three of my brothers.

During the horrific gunfight, a quick reaction force (QRF) of combined joint military personnel (including eight men from SEAL Team 10) were finally granted permission by Special Operations headquarters to launch. Upon reaching Sawtalo Sar, the United States QRF, which consisted of Two CH-47 Chinooks, two UH-60 Black Hawks and two AH-64 Apache attack helicopters started receiving small arms fire. During an attempt to insert my brothers from Team 10, one of Ahmad Shah's men fired a rocket-propelled grenade (RPG), which struck the transmission below the rear rotor assembly. This immediately caused the Chinook to plummet to the ground killing everyone inside.

Toward the end of the long firefight, Marcus was in and out of consciousness. He was miraculously found by a local Pashtun who carried him to his village, in accordance with the cultural tradition of Pashtunwali whereby asylum is offered to a person to protect them from their enemies. There, they dressed his wounds, fed him and protected him until U.S Coalition forces came to rescue him days later.

Before Marcus's rescue, the Afghani villagers strategically moved him from house to house to keep him safe from the Taliban forces that had come to finish him off.

(On a side note, I have heard plenty of people arm-chair quarterbacking the mission, saying they would have handled this mission much differently. But, in my opinion, no one has the right to critique their situation or the calls that were made that day. Those four courageous men did the best they could and fought gallantly to their death for our country and our freedom.)

Hostage Rescue. These missions are few and far between, but hostage rescues can be some of the most rewarding ones. In these cases, people are mostly just in the wrong place at the wrong time and find themselves in very dangerous, life threatening situations. The movie *Captain Phillips* or the news report on Jessica Buchanan in 2012 are both good examples of hostage rescue missions.

In April of 2009, merchant mariner Captain Richard Phillips was taken hostage by four pirates led by Abudwali Muse in the Indian Ocean. His vessel, the Maersk Alabama, was the sixth vessel in a week to be hijacked and the first vessel under the American flag to be successfully hijacked since the beginning of the 19th century. The spectacular rescue made by Team Six members was one for the history books.

Personal Security Detail (PSD). Here, SEALs operate as glorified bodyguards for high value dignitaries, visiting American political figures, foreign prime ministers of royalty, etc. The movie *Thirteen Hours* (about Benghazi) is a good portrayal of this type of assignment.

Direct Action (DA). These are probably the badass mission that most people think of when they think of what goes on in Special Forces. During a DA, we are "kicking down doors" and pulling potential threats off target. The operational tempo of this type of mission was very fast and often times, we'd only have minutes to throw on our gear and load the HUMMVS or birds (helicopters – primarily Chinooks or Blackhawks).

By far the most famous Direct Action mission to date was the Osama Bin Laden raid or *Operation Neptune Spear*. (*For those who don't know, Neptune's Spear is called the trident, which is what the SEAL's military insignia is called*). SEAL Team Six hit Bin Laden's fortified compound in Pakistan on May 2, 2011 just after 0100.

The entire mission was planned to take 40 minutes (including SSE) and the official time of the op was 38 minutes. But as it will, Murphy's Law kicked in and whatever could go wrong, did when one of the stealth Black Hawks clipped its tail rotor due to a dangerous airflow condition known as a "vortex ring state." No American forces were killed during the Op and it was yet another victory for the history books.

There are three modes of transportation we use in the SEAL teams during our missions:

1) Missions where we take HUMMVS are called Ground Attack Force (GAFs)

2) Attacks from the air are called Helo Attack Forces (HAFs)

3) Water borne missions were Boat Attack Forces (BAFs).

I have been on just one BAF in my career. We were *screaming* up the Tigris River in the Mark V boats operated by the Special Warcraft Combat Crewmen (SWCC). The boats were armed with twin 240 machineguns (which fired belt fed 7.62 rounds), .50 caliber machine guns and the Mk 47 ALGLs (automatic grenade launchers which fire the 40mm grenade rounds) mounted on the boats to provide ample protection for us.

While we were deployed, SEAL Team 10 went on roughly 78 combat missions in the six months that we were in Iraq in 2007. Most of those were Direct Action operations held in Baghdad and Sadr City in the middle of the night. On average each one took around 2-3 hours depending on the travel time and what type of intelligence we found on target.

I would venture to say that at least half of our DA missions were conducted in Sadr City, the city which, as you may recall, was Saddam Hussain's failed attempt at a housing project in the late 1990s.

At that time, Hussain had taken a one by one square mile plot of land and built hundreds of homes on it, housing more than 1 *million* people. (Yes, you read that correctly.)

Now, fast-forward to 2007, this hellhole had become a terrorist hotbed, and therefore, a SEAL playground. The conditions there were deplorable with much of the city without access to basic needs like clean water and electricity. The buildings were so dilapidated that we would often fall right through the roofs as we were trying to maintain the tactical advantage.

By the way, if you'd like to see a realistic portrayal of Sadr City, take a look at *The Long Road Home* on the National Geographic Channel. They do a good job of depicting what the city was like during the Operation Iraqi Freedom war on terrorism.

What made the missions in Sadr City particularly challenging was that we weren't just talking about a few bad guys. The culture of terror was being bred among the people who lived there – even children were being taught at very early ages to hate America. Anti-American propaganda littered the streets and it was simply just the way of life for them.

And those who weren't terrorists, enabled them out of fear and obligation because it was the only way they thought they could protect themselves and their families.

In other words, their values and perspectives were born out of terror and any decisions they made followed suit. Many knew no other way and would pass this same mentality along from generation to generation.

And in a city jam-packed with people, it was often difficult to discern the good from the bad. At the time, the Iraqi government allowed every family to own one AK 47. This meant a lot of people and a lot of weapons. As a matter of fact, I had several opportunities to kill people who were carrying their AK 47s, but didn't because they didn't pose an immediate threat. Instead, I would simply turn on my visible red laser on my PEQ-2 or ATPIAL and shine it on their chests to let them know US forces were in the area and to calmly go inside their house.

The different mission types I mentioned above obviously require an inordinate amount of preparation, extreme mental fortitude and toughness during the Ops themselves, and a deep-seeded value system upon which our training is built. The Teams have their own culture and value system, which produce, cultivate and replicate warriors of a certain breed who can endure excruciating pain and suffering in the face of adversity. Cultures like these – or any culture, in fact – thrive based on these types of deeply embedded values.

As SEALs, those values guide our system of beliefs, whether or not we think they do. Those beliefs impact our actions. And guess what? Your values also guide your beliefs, which ultimately impact your actions and decisions as well.

We're creatures of habit. I am. You are. So are the people of Sadr City.

But one bad decision, if left unchecked, could lead to disastrous results down the road.

And that's where the mental tools come into play.

If any of us had made decisions differently (good or bad) somewhere along the way, our *"now"* would look very different than it actually does today. There will always be positive or negative consequences for our actions and behaviors.

In the SEAL teams, if I was only a couple degrees off course in land navigation or diving, I could miss my target by dozens of meters or yards. And in that role, missing by a couple of meters or yards could have cost me my life or the lives of my brothers.

Hopefully, missing the mark for you doesn't mean there's a chance you'll die. BUT that doesn't mean there can't be fatalities along the way – for your marriage, relationship, family or job.

Let me break it down.

Oftentimes, as SEALs, our moral compasses can become distorted for whatever reasons and when this slow or sudden change occurs, it begins to affect what we value.

My moral compass shifted slowly during my first year in the Teams and I didn't course correct until some damaging decisions were made.

Luckily, I woke up and realized the path I was on led to isolation and devastation, so I reset my true North and got back on the right path.

It's a downward spiral. Once your values shift, those values begin to influence behavior, and eventually that behavior then influences your decisions. And, if left unchecked, our decisions determine your direction and ultimately your future.

This is also evident on much grander scales as well.

Sociologically speaking, the rise and fall of great societies are due to their ingrained values (or lack thereof). Likewise, cultures thrive due to deeply embedded values.

As humans, we are taught values (good or bad) at a very young age. Our values are what guide our beliefs, oftentimes without us even realizing it.

Next time you are in a seemingly endless or cyclical argument with your boss, spouse, kids, etc., ask yourself if it is possible that your values are clashing with theirs. You might stop thinking people are acting ridiculous if we learn what deep values are guiding their belief systems.

A person's values will guide them through life whether they realize it or not—what are your most important values?

We humans are creatures of habit and we are fairly predictable – whether or not you consider yourself predictable.

As part of our training in Advanced Special Operator Training (ASOT), Team guys are told to vary our routes to work, adjust our routines and modify our daily schedules so we don't become predicable to potential threats.

Your behavior and the decisions you make on a daily basis are largely determined by your beliefs. If you believe something about yourself or someone else (whether good or bad, true or untrue), you will begin to behave in a manner consistent with those beliefs.

For example, if you believe you are a victim, then you will act the victim. If you believe someone is powerless to change, then you will continue to enable them. If you grew up in a home that denigrated men, women, or people of certain races or ethnicities, then it is highly likely that you will wrestle with the same issues.

So, making this more practical, if you want to influence a person's behavior, you need to reach deeper to impact their beliefs.

As I mentioned earlier in the book, the divorce rate among Teams is as high as the attrition rate in BUD/S. Shocking and sad. Perhaps things could have been different if they were paying more attention to their moral compass.

Everyone, including SEALs, become complacent to change or are unwilling to grow, so their behaviors continue to blaze a trail of destruction in their lives. Over a period of time, our poor and selfish behaviors have a way of eroding relationships and our lives as a whole.

We need to be vigilant in guarding our minds (our beliefs) against negativity, pessimism and falsehood, because if we are not careful, our actions will become consistent with our beliefs. And, if left unchecked, we will wake up one day to realize the path we are on is lonely, empty and miserable.

Unfortunately, this is why many people during their last days on this planet have regrets. The legacies they leave behind are riddled with a trail of bad choices and wounded people. But if you are reading this and you are not on your death bed, it's not too late.

We have the power to choose everyday which path to take. Do you need to make a slight course correction in your life? If so, do it now before it is too late.

Set your compass accordingly and keep a tight rein on it to keep heading True North. Be prepared to the best of your ability for whatever comes your way. And make decisions based on what is *right*, not necessarily by the values that others expect you to hold.

Your direction, after all, determines your destiny.

CHAPTER 7

The Buck Stops Here

If you get on the wrong side of the right people, your career will be an uphill battle full of hardship.

The humid hot Arkansas weather was in full force in early July 2008.

Earlier that year, I had completed my land warfare block of training as part of SEAL Team 10's workup in Fort Chaffee.

It was there where I met my future wife and her three children.

As I've said before, SEALs work hard and play harder. So, one night, the boys and I decided to head to a dance club called The Cowboy in the neighboring town of Fort Smith. This town was our playground as my days came to an end.

The house lights were soon to come up and there she was. On the dance floor. It was ... instant attraction. And after a short five-month courtship that started that very night, we were married. We tried our hand at a long-distance relationship with her and her children in Fort Smith and me in Virginia Beach, Virginia. That was certainly not easy.

My platoon chief at the time suggested a transfer request to the Land Warfare division of TRADET, the training detachment of Naval Special Warfare, so I could be with my family.

Man, what a difficult decision. I wanted so badly to pursue the relationship with my future wife. But I also didn't want to abandon my brothers and leave them. After getting the support of the guys in my platoon – who were aware of the loss of Danielle – and praying about my decision, I reached out to my Command Master Chief (CMC) and requested the transfer.

My request was granted, and within a month, I was part of the SEAL cadre who trained other SEALs in Land Warfare. That didn't solve all of my problems though. See, my duty station was still there in Virginia Beach, so I couldn't move to Fort Smith. But, luckily, Land Warfare is the longest block of training for team guys before they are deployed, so I was able to spend five weeks at a time in Fort Smith/Fort Chaffee.

I also found out that we (the cadre) would conduct between four and five iterations of Land Warfare training per year for the various teams, meaning I would spend twenty to twenty-five weeks of the year with my wife and the kids.

I would also visit them on the weekends during my downtime.

I also chose to drive my personal vehicle (POV) from Virginia Beach to Fort Smith in order to give me some flexibility with my transportation because the cadre would stay on Fort Chaffee and use the government vehicles to drive on and off the base.

My POV, my 2007 Jeep Wrangler, didn't just help me, it also came in handy for carting guys around on base performing other duties.

It all looked good on paper, but there was a problem.

Two SEALs who were chiefs (E-7) of the Land Warfare cadre did not agree with my lateral transfer to TRADET division. And of course, if the CMC of SEAL Team 10 makes the call, then they have to obey the orders – but they secretly had it out for me.

I would later find out that these two made it their personal mission to get me "kicked out" of their division because they didn't like the reason for my transfer request.

Seems silly, right?

See, there's a motto in the Teams: First God, then Country, then Family.

They also knew that I was a man of faith and they despised that as well.

In their minds, I was breaking the code.

But personally, I don't see things that way. Never have. I place my wife and children above my job and career. Those are the values I was raised on.

The cards were stacked against me and I didn't even know it.

Not only that, but a short two months after I arrived at TRADET, they had assigned a new senior chief to be the head of that specific division. He didn't know any of my back story, but was quick to hop on the anti-Phillip bandwagon with the Land Warfare chiefs.

For the most part, I got along very well with my peers (the other E-5s and E-6s), but eventually word got around about the discord within the upper head-shed of the Land Warfare division. They wanted me out – for any reason.

Well, they eventually found what they were looking for.

Since I was using my POV for government use, I also thought it was okay to occasionally get gas on the base as well.

It was a little bit of a gray area for me. After all, I was also using my Jeep for government purposes, driving guys to and from the ranges and hauling supplies for example. Come to find out, government gas on the base was strictly for government vehicles.

As the beads of sweat dripped down my face from the morning's work, I drove up to the gas station there on base to fill it up for the week ahead. Halfway through the fill-up, both chiefs drove by in their government truck and stopped to ask what I was doing.

"Ummm ... getting gas?" I responded.

Immediately the yelling began, and I was ordered to follow them back to the barracks where we would talk to the senior chief.

Despite being only a three-minute drive, it was the longest ride of my life. The knot in my stomach was growing bigger by the second. I just knew something bad was about to happen.

I was told to stand outside the room at attention while they debriefed the senior chief in his room.

My heart was racing.

After about 15 minutes, the door flung open and I was ordered inside.

"Do you know why you're here?" one yelled.

"How many times have you filled your POV on base?" questioned another.

Rounds and rounds of these questions and whether or not I knew that it was illegal.

I stood accused of knowingly stealing government gas.

What's worse is that I couldn't even leave. I wasn't allowed to go back home. I was forced to stay there until they reached the NSW command the next day, at which point I was to drive back to Virginia Beach immediately.

Figuratively speaking, the train had left the station. There was no stopping it or slowing it down. These guys were determined to make an example out of me, and nothing was going to stop them.

Once I arrived in Virginia Beach, I felt such shame and regret around the decision. I recognized the severity of the situation and wished with all I had that I could change time and reverse the decision. I owned my mistake and apologized to all parties involved, but nothing seemed to suffice.

I remember thinking of the countless stories of bar fights, nights in jail, DUI's, failed piss tests and other debauchery that often went overlooked on the Teams and wondering why this case, over a mere $38 in gas, exacerbated into such a calamity?

I knew the answer.

In the SEAL Teams, if you get on the wrong side of the right people, your career will be an uphill battle full of hardship.

The decision at that point was to send me to Captain's Mast, where I was knocked down a rank.

But the train kept going.

The cadre had returned to Virginia Beach by this time and the two chiefs had recruited more people – whom I once considered allies – to join their campaign against me. My growing list of enemies went from being overseas to being right amongst my ranks.

At one point, I was put in front of a "Trident Board" full of enlisted chiefs and higher ranks, where I was grilled by a room of 35 Navy SEALS – all my superiors. The purpose was to grill me, intimidate me, and incite as much fear as they could.

I remember it like it was yesterday. I felt like a small child being reprimanded by the principal. I stood at attention for over an hour while being interrogated for a crime of just dollars in gas.

I said the only thing I could muster while feeling helpless, exposed and staring into the faces of 35 grown men. "I know you men have already made up your mind. So, at this point, it doesn't matter what I have to say."

Many shook their heads in agreement.

I wish I could say that I was the extreme rarity, but this kind of thing happens more often than not in the Teams.

If you recall, earlier in the book I talked about the "good ol' boys" club in the SEALs. This is what I'm talking about.

This kind of wolf pack mentality is what creates the extreme pressure to "fit in" and belong to culture of the team. It's easier, of course, to agree with the masses than risk estrangement because of different upbringing, values or beliefs.

The traumatizing event in front of the Trident Board, apparently was not enough to feed the fire burning in their bellies. I knew they'd be coming for more.

But when you corner a wolf, they have no choice but to fight back.

I gathered dozens of character references and letters of recommendation from other SEALs who had operated with me in years past.

I was then temporarily assigned to be in charge of the BUD/S candidates who lived there in Virginia Beach. These candidates were either out of high school or close to completing and just waiting to get a billet (slot) to go to BUD/S.

Though some might have seen that as a punishment, I genuinely enjoyed this type of training because I got to help young men improve their swimming skills and push them to achieve higher numbers in their physical screen tests.

Now, remember, at this point I was still engaged to be married and the wedding date was fast approaching. And they feasted their eyes on messing that up for me too.

My leave to take my honeymoon was denied – news that was personally delivered to me by one of the two main chiefs who started this whole mess. (I was even reprimanded for not asking to get married in the first place, if you can imagine that.)

When the news was delivered, I happened to have a Nerf ball in my hand. Out of anger, I threw the ball against the wall. The bearer of bad news later tried to press assault charges against me for "throwing a Nerf ball."

You heard me. *Assault by a Nerf ball.*

A pathetic and cowardly move, if you ask me.

The laughable charge obviously fell flat, but it's a shining example of the lack of character and integrity that these few men had. And worse, the pack just went along with it, without one single sole questioning the validity of the claim.

A month passed, when I got word that the Commanding Officer (CO) of Group Two wanted to have a meeting with me. When this happens in the Navy, it is either really, really good news, or really, really bad.

Guess which it was?

I stepped into his office with my dress blues, sweating profusely as I stood at attention. And mind you, those uniforms don't breathe.

The CO recounted how he had been approached by the two chiefs and a senior enlisted SEAL to remove my Trident. My chest hurt as I felt my heart ripping in two.

He seemed like a fair and down-to-earth man though and he was my last sliver of hope that true justice was going to be served.

But despite my impeccable record in the Navy, my high marks and superior performance evaluations, my letters of recommendation and character references (which, by the way, I was later told by a trusted source had mysteriously disappeared and never made it to the CO), I was instructed that if I stayed in the Navy, my Trident would be removed.

Unbelievable.

You know those times when it seems like life is just gunning for you? When nothing makes sense and it all feels like a bad dream? This was one of those times.

I went home with my head hung low.

It was true. I was steamrolled.

Once the "train left the station" at the gas pump on that hot day in Arkansas, nothing could stop it from charging down the track at full speed.

What I did *was* wrong – I am owning that – and a tremendous life lesson for me.

As Carl Lentz, Lead Pastor of Hillsong NYC, wrote in his book, The Moment,"We have all made mistakes that we regret and would choose to do over if we had the chance. We all have stories, we all have a past and the difference between people who are effective and who are not is this: Will you use your story, or will your story use you? When you reflect on your life, what do you remember most? Do you look back at all the misses and mistakes and all the stuff you didn't do?"

The way my situation was handled was wrong and grossly unjust. In fact, it caught the attention of several of our support personnel there at the Group Two Command. One chief, a Yeoman, actually approached me at one point saying that in his 16 years in the Navy, he had never seen anything like my case. He expressed his deep condolences with a look of disbelief in his eyes.

He let me know that the legal option was available to me to go to the Navy's legal department that helps falsely accused and mistreated servicemen have a voice and receive representation. Though I pursued it – and discovered that mine was a prime case for such a legal matter – it was my Plan B.

My Plan A was to pursue getting out of the Navy all together.

I knew it was a shot in the dark, but I was reach and fighting for the light at my dark and unjust tunnel. There was no way I was going to end up on a ship doing God-knows-what. That just wasn't me.

At this point, I still had three years left on my reenlistment and I knew it would take a miracle to get me out.

Well, as He always has, God showed up and answered my prayers again.

For the first time in 23 years, the Navy just happened to be downsizing and my request to get out was approved under one stipulation: If I repaid my bonus (which at the time was around $60,000) that I received when I reenlisted in Baghdad for five years, my separation from the Navy would be approved.

Thus, in August 2009, I was honorably discharged from the Navy as a Special Warfare Operator Third Class Petty Officer (SO3).

I love the metaphor of a car as it relates to our lives. There is a reason that the rearview mirror is much smaller than the windshield. It's there so you can glance at what's behind you while continuing to stay focused on what's ahead.

Remember, true leaders don't live in the past. They may glance at it to learn from it, but the future is too important to waste a single moment worrying or even thinking about what can't be changed.

I wish there was a piece of gear in my Go Bag that allowed me to go back and make different decisions. There's no gear for that though.

I guess that's why in the SEALs we train so exclusively. We make mistakes in training in order to minimize the mistakes made down range – because the price tag on those mistakes are far too costly.

CHAPTER 8

The Journey Forward

Our lives are a culmination of our choices and the choices made for us by others (the good, bad and ugly) and what we do with those choices determines who and what we will become in the future.

After being honorably discharged in August of 2009, I picked up a contractor job with NEK Services as a Sensitive Site Exploitation (SSE) instructor and moved across the country to Fayetteville, North Carolina.

The simplest way to describe SSE it to liken it to shows like CSI, but instead of calculating blood spatter patterns to determine bullet trajectory, we would full investigate a target as soon as it was secured.

So, my job was to develop training materials and fully mock scenarios to teach the Green Berets the proper techniques to exploit the target – a unique and vital skill.

The mock scenarios would usually go down like this: Once the call "Target is secure, Commence SSE" comes in over our MBITTER radios, we rapidly switch gears from neutralizing the threat to systematically turning the target inside out.

Our white lights go on so we can look for caches of weapons, bomb materials, buried weapons, false walls, etc. We also begin the process of questioning our detainees with the help of our interpreters.

This is probably a good time to mention that there are only two types of subject matter experts (SME) who roll on target with us:

1- **Explosive Ordinance Disposal (EOD)** guys are worth their weight in gold. For lack of a better definition, they operate as the Navy's bomb squad. They can dismantle pressure plates, trip wires, improvised explosive devices (IEDs), mines or any sort of booby traps set up by the bad guys. These folks don't go through BUD/S, but have an intense (more mental and psychologically rigorous) training process. During my time in my first platoon, I became very close with the EOD operator assigned to us. He would often attend and go through our training to give him a general idea of what to expect when he was operating with us overseas.

2- **Interpreters**, like the EOD guys, are extremely helpful in assisting us in our tactical questioning during SSE and can be ...well ... let's just say "motivating" when questioning potential terrorists. Even though the Navy and other military branches have their own separate language school that men and women can attend, we typically used vetted local interpreters who spoke the local dialects of Farsi, Arabic or Pashtu.

During SSE, we also take the biometrics of potential detainees – this includes fingerprint and retinal scans – that are then broadcast in real-time via satellite to the U.S. databases. Within minute, intel comes back to us on whether or not the people we are interrogating are already in the database ("bad guys," in other words). If they're not already in the database, we'll get as much information from them as possible and then send them on their way. On the other hand, if they come back as a hit, they are boarded onto the HUMMVEEs or Helios for a little jaunt with us back to the Green Zone where they are turned over to the CIA for further investigation.

The last part of SSE was to try and get as much information as possible from cell phones, laptops and computers. Today's technology has advanced so much that we can now retrieve all the information out of these devices and leave virtually no digital signature. Contacts, texts, emails, pictures, etc. all prove extremely valuable in creating additional target packages.

Now obviously, I can't go into much more detail given Operations Security (OPSEC) reasons but rest assured we get everything we want.

Thus, all the information gathered during the SSE process, which can often take between 30 and 45 minutes, can lead to other "follow-on" targets. And, if time allows (meaning, we're still under the cover of darkness) and the information we gather is time sensitive enough, we will roll onto other targets that evening or early morning.

I was assigned on the SSE contract for just over a year when it just came time for me to make a big shift in my life – to shift occupations all together.

See, there was this church called the Vineyard that I would attend whenever I went home on leave to visit family. As it turned out, they were hiring for a full-time Community Life Pastoral position.

Me? An ordained pastor?

Crazy, right?

It seemed that way to me too. I mean, how does a guy go from a Navy SEAL to a pastor?

But something – *something* – felt right very right about it. Like it was a good fit.

Perhaps this was God's way of moving me from the physical war over power to the spiritual war over people's souls.

After all, if there's one Biblical concept I understand, it's spiritual warfare.

Think of the tactics of a terrorist – crafty, deceitful and deadly – the same tactics that draw you into sin.

Following a slew of psychological tests, references and interviews, I joined the Vineyard Cincinnati pastoral staff.

I love people and highly value relationships, and the thought of protecting their souls brought me great joy – so this didn't seem like a job at all.

As a leader of a small group ministry, I spent my days providing oversight for over 1,500 people in the southern greater Cincinnati area. I partnered with three other remarkable men in that specific area of the ministry, and together, we were our own unique "fire team."

There was still something missing though. I needed something that gave me an outlet and allowed me to be more demonstrative and passionate.

Well, God once again answered my prayers when he opened a door for me to be the football Chaplain for the University of Cincinnati.

Butch Jones invited me to come and speak to the men during their training camp at Higher Ground. We all had a blast that evening and the team welcomed me with open arms.

From that moment forward, I became enmeshed with the team as I led prayers, times of scripture reading, Bible studies, chapel times before games, and yelling a few profanities on the field.

I guess you could say I morphed into a coach of my own, using my background and stories to motivate and inspire the people before me who were on their journeys to become men.

Unfortunately, about two years into my pastoral position, the failing economy caught up with the church. I heard that several bank loans were being renewed at higher rates and ultimately, the church was faced with eliminating twenty staff positions (accounting for close to one million dollars per year).

Now, keep in mind, the Vineyard Cincinnati was (and still is) considered a "mega" church in which weekend attendance reached close to 6,000 people. There were over one hundred people on staff who made all the logistical cogs in the giant wheel turn smoothly.

As I'm sure you have figured by now, my number was up and my position was one of the ones cut. It was equally difficult for my father, who was on the board of trustees for the church and part of the decision-making process. But since I was one of the last hired, I was one of the first let go. They actually cut our ministry in half, which was the largest cut to a single department.

It was, no doubt, a sobering time in my life. But something inside whispered to me that everything would be okay.

My first biological son, Zadak, was born in April 2011, so he was just over a year old when all of this went down.

So, there I was, a father of four children, a husband, and unemployed.

Just when our severance package ran out and our savings was getting dangerously low, another door opened for us in Aurora, Colorado when I was accepted as the Community Life Pastor at the Smoky Hill Vineyard. And after going through the same rigorous hiring process that I went through before, I moved my family across the country for our new life and a new adventure.

Oh yeah, and my wife was pregnant with Briah – my first biological daughter. Picture it. Family of six moving across the country. Big fun.

We were warmly embraced by a very inviting crew at Smoky Hill Vineyard.

The position was similar to my previous one, so the workload and the description were familiar.

I doubled the size of the small group ministry and started a men's ministry as well. Even though the senior leadership and I had a similar vision for where we were headed, we disagreed on how to get there. Ultimately, we all decided it was time to move on, and I was getting the nudge to make another shift in career direction.

By this time, I had held my position for twenty months and there was really only one option that made sense – it was time for me to go back to school.

Wait, what? (If this were an 80s movie, you would have heard the soundtrack playing in the background scratch to a halt.)

I hated school.

As a matter of fact, I was probably the ONLY guy in boot camp who did not want to take advantage of the Montgomery G.I. Bill. At the time, all I knew was that I had my undergraduate degree in Marketing and that I'd had enough of school.

Turns out, the Post-911 G.I. Bill is pretty amazing. Not only could I go back to school on the government's dime, but I was also qualified to receive a basic allowance for housing (BAH) which paid our mortgage. Somehow, we made the finances work, but rubbing two nickels together hoping to get more money sure was hard work!

My wife also wanted to go back to school to get her Masters' degree, so we found a way to make ends meet. We both got accepted to Denver Seminary where I was working toward a Masters' Degree in Leadership and she was earning hers in Christian Studies.

I had to attend full-time in order to maximize my G.I. Bill and for my wife to qualify for half off of her tuition.

Since I'm a kinesthetic learner by nature, sitting in a sterile class room for hours on end was challenging enough.

But now add to it the hours of required reading that my credit hours required. Trust me, I did the math. Sixty-two credit hours totaling 31,000 pages of reading and 930 pages of writing! Ugh!

No wonder I dragged my heels so much on writing this book. I'm *still* exhausted even though I graduated in Spring of 2016.

Even though I am not currently employed in a typical "leadership" role, I have the daily opportunity to exercise the principles I have learned.

For example, if you can't lead yourself, then how can you expect to lead anyone else?

Leading ourselves is a life-long lesson to be learned. One filled with humility, sacrifice, honesty and hard work. Being a leader out front can oftentimes be a lonely position. Being the one primarily responsible for decisions, knowing it is impossible to please everyone all the time and receiving copious amounts of criticism by others is not necessarily a sexy job description. The role of a leader comes at a high cost and not many can shoulder the responsibilities. I am gratefully given the opportunity to lead and influence others in my occupation — a responsibility I don't take lightly.

Currently, I am speaking full-time and leading an active shooter class in Jeffersonville, Ohio. I teach this class to give others a unique, once-in-a-lifetime opportunity to develop their tactical mindset and skillset on a live fire range, pushing their abilities to the limit.

I love teaching others how to use their tactical brain – it can help them succeed and, in some cases, save lives. As a matter of fact, three months after completing the course, one of my student's homes was broken into. With the skills and confidence he had gained, he was able to effectively and efficiently handle the situation. He kept his family safe and tactically sound. It can happen to anyone, anywhere.

But above all else, being a father is the most rewarding thing I have ever done. I love being a Dad. Zadak and Briah light up my life and we have so much fun together – whether it's jumping on a trampoline, playing with LEGOs, cuddling while watching movies, going to the park or building forts at home.

I am extremely fluent in the language of *play*.

The time and personal investment men can make in their children's lives will page huge dividends in their futures.

It's hard as hell sometimes. Believe me, I get it. But hang in there.

If I may be so bold ... when faced with the choice to choose time with your kids or something else for yourself, you have to choose your kids the majority of the time. The reward is not immediate and most times it takes years and years to see the fruit of your investment in their lives. But it is *so* worth it.

I will always be "Dad," but I have a long road ahead of me as I embark upon new adventures, but one thing is for sure— I will always be on the go and living life to the fullest.

Many team guys who get out just want to settle down somewhere quiet and live a simple life. Some are among you in your workplaces as teachers, engineers, financial planners, etc.

I get why some would want that, but that's simply not me.

No matter where we land, though, we will always be the silent warriors we were trained to be.

Most don't seek glory or even like talking about our time in the teams and what we did.

We blend in.

But make no mistake, if the stuff ever hits the fan and the world begins to figuratively turn upside down, it's always nice to be friends with one.

Maybe that's a good thing to add to your Go Bag.

PHOTOS

Top: L-R: Danielle and Phillip; Phillip's pinning ceremony.
Bottom: Eric, Phillip posing with Frogman.

EXERCISES

Now that you've read *The Truth Behind My Trident*, let's work on the ways that you can overcome some of your own obstacles the Navy SEAL way.

I. In chapter 5, I gave the analogy of sitting on a fence with a dog on either side – a good dog and a bad dog. Every choice we make in life feeds one dog or the other, and the one who gets fed the most will ultimately defeat the other.

What choices have you made in your life and your business that feed the bad dog?

_____

_____

_____

_____

_____

What choices have you made in your life and your business that feed the good dog?

_____

_____

_____

_____

_____

_____

What can you do, either day-to-day or in the long-term, to change the pattern of feeding the bad dog?

_____

_____

_____

_____

_____

_____

_____

II. Think about your short-and long-term goals in life or in business. What are the top five things you are trying to achieve?

1.

_____

_____

2.

_____

_____

3.

_____

_____

4.

_____

_____

5.

_____

_____

III. Now, let's think about your Go Bag and the tools you have in your arsenal to overcome the obstacles in your everyday life and your business.

a. What are the negative or self-defeating thoughts that keep you from achieving your goals?

_____

_____

_____

_____

_____

_____

_____

_____

b. My Kevlar helmet protected my head from gunshots and explosives that I faced when up against the enemy. What do you have in your Go Bag that will protect your mind from explosive confrontations or self-defeating thoughts in your personal and professional life?

_____

_____

_____

_____

_____

_____

_____

_____

c. What are some of the things that get in the way of your mental, physical and spiritual success?

_____

_____

_____

_____

_____

_____

_____

d. My body armor protected my heart and vital organs when faced with conflicts in the battlefield. What components do you have in place to protect your heart – your spirit – when reaching for your goals?

_____

_____

_____

_____

e. Are there things going on in your life that prevent you from proactively achieving your goals? If so, what are they?

_____

_____

_____

_____

_____

f. My H-Gear not only held the things that protected me, but also carried the tools I could use to fight offensively fight back against any threat I came up against. What is in your Go Bag to help you stand up to threats and stay on track to complete your mission? *Remember, your proactive tools can include your faith, friends or hobbies.*

_____
_____
_____
_____
_____
_____
_____

g. My boots allowed me to persevere by keeping me grounded and allowing me to focus on things one step at a time. What are some of your step-by-step goals and what is in your Go Bag that will help you achieve them?

_____
_____
_____
_____
_____
_____
_____

h. What are some of the ways that your peers or your culture is influencing how you live your best life personally or professionally?

_____
_____
_____
_____

i. My uniform was my second skin. It identified who I was and what I stood for. What are the identifiers in your life that tell people who you are and what you are about. And are you comfortable with those identifiers?

_____
_____
_____
_____
_____

j. My helo lanyard was a small piece of fabric that connected me to the helicopter to ensure that I was securely fastened. What do you have in your Go Bag that ensures that stay safely anchored in turbulent times?

_____
_____
_____
_____

k. What are some of the emotional enemies you face in achieving your goals?

_____

_____

_____

_____

_____

_____

_____

_l. As a Navy SEAL, we put certain rounds in our weapons in order to accomplish the mission or task in front of us. What emotional or spiritual ammunition do you have in your Go Bag that you can use against things like fear, shame, gossip, rumors, etc.?

_____

_____

_____

_____

_____

_____

_____

ABOUT THE AUTHOR

Phillip Koontz is a former Navy SEAL of six years who was honorably discharged in 2009.

Following his time as a SEAL, Phillip went from Fire Team leader to spiritual leader when he stepped into full-time ministry as a Community Life Pastor in The Vineyard church. After four years of ministry, he embarked upon a new journey during which he completed his Masters' Degree in Leadership from Denver Seminary in 2016.

He is now a motivational speaker who has presented at hundreds of events both nationally and internationally, covering topics such as team-building, conflict resolution, overcoming adversity and building mental toughness. Phillip has appeared on television, held webinars and mentored several pre-BUD/S candidates. He is also the founder of Tactical Advantage Consulting (TAC) a high impact, live fire, active shooter course held in Columbus, Ohio.

Phillip held the volunteer role as Ohio Regional Manager for Destiny Rescue, a non-profit organization which rescues, restores, and protects children trapped in sexual exploitation and slavery.

He has two children, Zadak and Briah, and currently lives in Monument, Colorado.

Made in the USA
Columbia, SC
22 March 2023

14114233R10070